Built, Not Born

The New Rules of Money, Confidence, and Power

Michelle Ward

Harbor & Ink Press

Published by Harbor & Ink Press

First Edition, 2025
Cover design and interior formatting by Harbor & Ink Press.

Contents

Foreword

By Dr. Alexandra Hayes, CFP®, AFC®, PhD (Behavioral Finance)
Financial Psychologist • Certified Financial Planner™ • Accredited Financial Counselor®
Director of Behavioral Finance Research, The American Institute for Financial Wellness

For more than twenty years, my work has centered on one essential truth:

Financial transformation begins long before a budget is ever written.

It begins in the mind.

As a financial psychologist and behavioral finance researcher, I have spent my career studying the emotional, cognitive, and behavioral patterns that shape how women think, feel, and act with money. I have worked with clients ranging from corporate executives to single mothers rebuilding their lives from the ground up. Despite their different circumstances, they all share one common challenge:

They were never taught the *psychology* of money—only the mechanics.

That is why **Built, Not Born** is such a significant and necessary contribution.

Michelle Ward has created a program that aligns precisely with what decades of research—and thousands of real-world cases—have consistently shown us:

lasting financial change requires self-awareness, behavioral structure, and small, repeatable actions.

Not perfection.

Not wealth to begin with.

And certainly not complicated systems.

The brilliance of this book lies in its accessibility. It is grounded in science, yet deeply human. Michelle translates complex financial and psychological concepts into clear, empowering steps that any woman can follow—regardless of where she is starting.

The 30-day blueprint she presents mirrors the exact sequence I use in both clinical and coaching environments:

Identifying your money story

Interrupting the emotional patterns that drive unhelpful habits

Building systems that support sustainable behavior change

Strengthening confidence through small, consistent wins

Creating structure *before* strategy

Michelle does not merely understand this process—she has lived it. Her journey from starting with nothing to building a thriving publishing business and financial foundation gives this work an authenticity that cannot be manufactured.

Most financial books focus on knowledge.

This one focuses on transformation.

Most books tell you what to do.

This one shows you how to do it in a way your brain can actually sustain.

In a landscape crowded with oversimplified advice and one-size-fits-all formulas, **Built, Not Born** stands out as one of the few resources that genuinely aligns with the research on behavioral change and emotional wellbeing.

If you commit to the next thirty days with honesty and curiosity, this book will not only reshape your finances—it will reshape the beliefs that have guided your financial life for years.

And that is where real wealth begins.

I am honored to introduce Michelle Ward's work to you, and even more honored by what it will unlock for every woman who picks up this book.

Your relationship with money is about to evolve.

And with it, so will your life.

— Dr. Alexandra Hayes, CFP®, AFC®, PhD (Behavioral Finance)

Preface: Built in Silence

Most people only see the ending of a transformation.

They see the confidence once it's visible.

The momentum once it's undeniable.

The results once they can be measured, shared, or explained.

What they don't see is the long stretch before that — the part where you keep going without any proof that it's working.

That's the part I know best.

Not long ago, my son said something to me that stopped me in my tracks. He looked at what I was doing and said, *"It feels like you got successful really quickly."*

I remember smiling, because I understood why it looked that way.

What he was seeing was the highlight reel.

What he hadn't seen were the years before that — the quiet work, the learning curve, the false starts, the days where progress didn't show up in any obvious way. The moments where I kept showing up anyway, long before there was anything to point to and say, *"See? It worked."*

That's the thing about success. Most people only ever see about five percent of it.

They see the outcome, not the repetition.

The confidence, not the doubt.

The visible win, not the invisible discipline that made it possible.

Every person who's built something meaningful knows this. The real work happens long before anyone notices.

There were long periods where I was doing the work quietly. Learning how money actually worked. Unlearning beliefs that kept me anxious, reactive, or stuck. Building systems that felt boring on good days and exhausting on bad ones. I wasn't sharing progress. I wasn't being cheered on. Most of the time, I wasn't even sure I was making progress at all.

From the outside, it probably looked like nothing was happening.

Inside, everything was shifting.

I was still paying bills. Still second-guessing myself. Still feeling that familiar knot in my chest when something unexpected came up. But slowly — almost imperceptibly — my reactions changed. I paused before spending. I stopped avoiding my numbers. I made calmer decisions, even when I didn't feel confident making them.

Not because I suddenly believed in myself.

But because I had structure to fall back on.

Motivation came and went. Confidence followed much later. What stayed was repetition — showing up on ordinary days, sticking with simple systems, and choosing consistency over intensity when I was tired, discouraged, or doubting myself.

There were many moments where it would have been easier to stop. To decide it wasn't working fast enough. To assume I just wasn't "one of those people" who felt calm or capable with money.

What kept me going wasn't belief.

It was commitment — to small, unglamorous actions that didn't require enthusiasm or certainty. Actions that worked quietly, in the background, long before they produced visible results.

This is why I don't believe financial confidence is something you're born with.

It's something you build — patiently, imperfectly, and often without witnesses.

If you're reading this while doing all the "right things" but still wondering why it feels slow...

If you're showing up without applause...

If you're questioning whether the effort is worth it because nothing looks different yet...

You are not failing.

You are building.

This book exists because I needed something like it in that season — something honest, practical, and steady. Not another promise of quick fixes or dramatic breakthroughs. Just a way forward that respected real life, real emotions, and real limitations.

Everything that follows is designed to support you in the quiet work.

Not to push you.

Not to rush you.

But to help you stay.

Because staying — especially when no one is watching — is where everything actually changes.

What follows is the structure that helped me stay when nothing looked like it was working.

How to Use This Book

This isn't the kind of book you read once, nod along to, and forget.

This is a book you live with — one you return to whenever your money feels messy, your confidence wavers, or you need to reconnect with the calm, grounded, capable version of yourself.

Inside these pages, you'll find a deliberate blend of two essential elements.

Emotional Insight

So, you can understand the stories, patterns, and beliefs quietly shaping your financial life — often more powerfully than any spreadsheet ever could.

Practical Guidance

So, you can build real, steady confidence with money through simple tools, frameworks, and step-by-step strategies that actually fit your life.

Together, these elements are designed to move you beyond theory and into meaningful, sustainable change.

The 30-Day Reset Steps

At the end of most chapters, you'll find a signature feature that anchors this entire book: **The 30-Day Reset Steps**.

These short, focused actions are the heart of the work.

Each Reset Step invites you to *embody* the chapter's lesson — not just think about it. They're intentionally simple, but deeply effective, because confidence grows through repetition, and meaningful change happens through small actions taken consistently.

You don't need to overhaul your life overnight.

You just need to keep showing up.

Getting the Most Out of This Book

Read in order.

Each chapter builds on the last, guiding you from emotional awareness to practical mastery — from your past money story to your future financial identity.

Don't rush the process.

Yes, you could read this book in a weekend. But transformation happens when you pause, reflect, and practice. Give yourself permission to slow down and engage fully.

Use the Reset Steps as a personal program.

You can work through them chapter by chapter or focus on the areas where you need the most support right now. There is no single "right" way to move through this work.

Return to the resets whenever life shifts.

A career change. A relationship transition. A setback. A breakthrough. Any major life change can unsettle your financial foundation. Let the Reset Steps be your realignment tool.

Make it your own.

Not every exercise will resonate equally — and that's okay. Adapt them to your personality, your lifestyle, and your goals. What matters most is that you stay in motion.

This Book Is Your Companion — Not Your Critic

Every page is designed to support you, not judge you.

Financial wellbeing is about far more than numbers. It's about clarity, peace, stability, and the freedom to build a life that feels rich in every sense of the word.

Reader's Roadmap

This book is divided into three core parts, followed by a bonus section designed to help you integrate and expand on what you've learned. Each chapter blends emotional insight with practical tools and concludes with a Reset Step to help you turn understanding into action.

PART ONE: Understanding Your Money Story

Chapter 1 — Rethinking Money: It's More Than Numbers
Chapter 2 — The Messy Middle
Chapter 3 — The Generational Echo: How Family Stories Shape Your Wallet
Chapter 4 — The Psychology of Money

Here, you'll uncover the roots of your habits, fears, and financial patterns — so you can finally rewrite the story that has been running your money life.

PART TWO: Building Your Financial Foundation

Chapter 5 — Your Financial Inventory: Where Are You Now?
Chapter 6 — The Financial Therapy Toolkit
Chapter 7 — Budgeting That Works — For You

Chapter 8 — Debt & Credit: Facing the Past, Shaping the Future
Chapter 9 — Saving & Investing: Building Stability and Growth

In this section, you'll organize your financial world, heal old money wounds, and create systems that support you — rather than stress you.

PART THREE: Navigating Change & Sustaining Success

Chapter 10 — Financial Transitions: Career, Family & Life Changes
Chapter 11 — Sustaining Success: Healing, Habits & Long-Term Confidence

Conclusion — Your Roadmap Forward

This final section focuses on resilience — helping you move through life's inevitable ups and downs with clarity, stability, and grounded strength.

Bonus Section: From Foundation to Expansion

After the core journey, you'll find a **bonus masterclass-style section** designed to help you consolidate what you've built and look forward with intention. This includes deeper reflection, integration tools, and a **Wealth Identity Declaration** to help you articulate — and own — the financial identity you're creating.

You'll also find **resources and further reading** to support continued growth long after the final page.

One Last Thing

At the end of each chapter, you'll find a Reset Step — a simple daily action designed to help you live the chapter's lesson.

Think of these resets as building blocks: small, repeatable actions that compound into lasting financial confidence.

You don't need perfection.

You don't need to get everything right.

You only need to take it one day, one step, one reset at a time.

Introduction. This Is Something You Build

If you've ever promised yourself, you'd *finally* get on top of your finances—only to end up right back where you started—this isn't a failure of willpower or intelligence.

It's human.

Most women don't struggle with money because they lack discipline. They struggle because traditional financial advice is overwhelming, overly complicated, or built for someone else's life entirely.

What we actually need is something different:

A system that feels clear.

A rhythm that feels doable.

A reset that *sticks*—even when life gets busy, emotional, unpredictable, or messy.

That is exactly what **Built, Not Born: A 30-Day Blueprint to Transform Your Money Mindset and Build the Life You've Imagined** is designed to give you.

This isn't a book you skim, nod along to, and forget. It's a guided experience you move through—one that reshapes not only how you manage money, but how you think, feel, and show up in your financial life.

How the Reset Works

The Reset unfolds over four focused weeks, each designed to shift a different layer of your financial world.

Week One — Awareness & Mindset

You'll uncover your money story, long-held beliefs, emotional triggers, and the hidden habits driving your financial decisions—often without your awareness.

Week Two — Spending with Intention

You'll create a realistic, supportive budget that reflects your *real* life—not a rigid or idealised version of it.

Week Three — Debt & Credit Clarity

You'll face debt without shame, understand credit with confidence, and build a repayment approach that feels empowering rather than punishing.

Week Four — Saving & Growing Wealth

You'll strengthen your financial foundation, build a safety net, and take your first calm, confident steps toward investing and long-term growth.

Each chapter gives you clear language, grounded tools, and practical strategies aligned with that week's focus.

And at the end of every chapter, you'll find your **daily Reset Step**—thirty simple actions, one for each day, designed to turn insight into habit.

Some steps invite reflection.
Others ask for clear, decisive action.
All of them are intentionally small enough to follow through on—yet powerful enough to change your momentum.

Why This Works

As the author of multiple bestselling personal finance books read by thousands of women worldwide, I've learned one essential truth:

Information alone doesn't create transformation.
Integration does.

Lasting financial change happens when two elements come together:

Understanding the psychology behind your money decisions

Building practical systems that support new behaviour

Built, Not Born works because it connects the two.

It helps you understand *why* you do what you do—and then gives you a structured, realistic way to do things differently.

By the end of thirty days, you will have:

A budget you can actually maintain

A debt plan that feels manageable

A growing savings foundation

Your first confident steps toward investing

And most importantly:

A calmer, clearer, more empowered relationship with money.

Whether you're starting from scratch, rebuilding after setbacks, or stepping into your next level, this Reset meets you exactly where you are.

The Real Beginning

Before we talk about budgets, spreadsheets, or payoff strategies, we begin somewhere deeper—with your relationship to money itself.

Because lasting financial change has never started with numbers.

It has always started with *you*.

So here is your invitation:

Commit to the next thirty days.

Show up for yourself in small, meaningful ways.

Release perfection—and choose consistency instead.

One day.

One step.

One reset at a time.

This isn't about being born confident with money.

It's about building it—intentionally, patiently, and on your own terms.

Your new money story begins now.

Chapter One

Rethinking Money — It's More Than Numbers

Most of us are taught to see money as a simple equation of income, expenses, and savings. Budgets, spreadsheets, and calculators are supposed to hold the answers. But if it were truly that straightforward, far fewer people would struggle with finances. The truth is that beneath the surface of dollars and cents lies something far more powerful: the emotional, cultural, and psychological forces that quietly shape our decisions.

Consider a young professional who diligently tracks expenses, saves a portion of every paycheck, and avoids obvious financial mistakes—yet still feels stuck. This isn't a failure of math. It's a reflection of the invisible beliefs, habits, and emotions driving their behavior. Hidden narratives—often learned in childhood—continue to play out long into adulthood, steering choices even when logic points elsewhere.

Recognizing that money is more than numbers allows us to peel back the layers of inherited attitudes and emotional triggers. In this chapter, we'll uncover how family messages, cultural scripts, and unconscious habits create your personal "money story." By bringing these into the light, you'll begin to understand where your financial behaviors truly come from—and how to change them.

Money Beliefs Uncovered

Our relationship with money begins long before we ever earn a paycheck. Childhood memories, family routines, and even silence around the subject lay the foundation for how we view money as adults.

Think back: Did your parents argue about bills at the kitchen table? Did one caregiver emphasize saving every cent while another spent freely? Maybe money was never discussed at all—leaving you to fill in the blanks with your own assumptions. Every experience leaves an imprint.

One child might grow up in a household where pocket money was encouraged and saving accounts were opened early. Another might witness financial secrecy, with parents whispering behind closed doors about overdue bills. These early experiences become scripts that run quietly in the background, shaping your comfort with spending, saving, or risk-taking.

Even cultural background plays a part. Some communities normalize open conversation about money, while others treat it as taboo. Some cultures emphasize generosity and shared wealth; others prioritize caution and self-preservation. Whatever the messages, they become the "rules" we unconsciously carry into adulthood.

Family "money rules" often feel arbitrary but leave lasting impressions:

- A parent who demanded saving every coin may instill fear of spending.
- A grandparent who survived hard times might pass down a mindset of scarcity.

- Caregivers who argued about debt may make financial discussions feel unsafe.

Over time, these conflicting lessons weave together into a complex personal money story. They whisper unspoken judgments about what feels "right" or "wrong" when it comes to spending, saving, giving, or hiding money.

Scarcity vs. Abundance

When left unexamined, early lessons can become self-fulfilling patterns. A scarcity mindset develops when someone believes there will never be enough—no matter their current reality. Scarcity thinkers often hoard resources, avoid opportunities, and obsess over small expenses. They might work jobs they dislike simply because leaving feels too risky. Anxiety, guilt, and fear become constant companions.

On the other end of the spectrum lies an abundance mindset: the belief that resources can be created, opportunities discovered, and risks survived. People with this outlook tend to invest in their skills, start side projects, or pivot careers, trusting in their resilience. Anxiety loosens its grip, replaced by curiosity and optimism.

Think of the friend who finally left a stable but unfulfilling job to pursue a passion project—and succeeded. That's abundance in action. Their willingness to trust themselves and adapt opened the door to growth.

Reflection Exercise

Start uncovering your own beliefs by asking yourself:

- What's my earliest memory involving money?
- How did my family talk about—or avoid talking about—fi-

nances?

- Did I grow up seeing fear, secrecy, generosity, or pride around money?

Write your answers in a journal. As themes emerge, notice which beliefs still serve you and which may be holding you back. Awareness is the first step toward change.

Emotions and Your Wallet

Finances are rarely about numbers alone. Once you've started uncovering your money stories, the next step is to notice how emotions sneak into everyday decisions. Even the smallest financial choices—splitting a bill, swiping at the checkout, or paying a utility online—are colored by what you're feeling in the moment.

Stress, guilt, or shame don't vanish when you open a banking app. They show up in subtle ways: in the hesitation before clicking "submit payment," in the relief of a purchase that wasn't planned, or in the knot in your stomach when you see a balance lower than expected.

Picture a stressful workweek. You come home exhausted and, without thinking, order takeout or add random items to an online cart. For someone else, that same stress might cause them to avoid logging into their banking app entirely. The emotions drive the behavior, not the numbers.

The tricky part is that money carries so much symbolic weight. A new pair of shoes isn't just leather and laces—it can be a reward, a confidence boost, or a distraction from loneliness. The same is true in reverse: skipping a night out with friends to "save money" isn't always about the $40 dinner. It might be about guilt, fear of scarcity, or worry about judgment.

Awareness of this emotional undercurrent is the foundation for change. Instead of shaming yourself for an "impulse buy" or procrastinating on a payment, pause and ask: *What was I feeling right before I made this choice?* That simple question can reveal patterns that logic alone never could.

Fight, Flight, or Freeze with Finances

When stress shows up, our nervous system responds in familiar ways: fight, flight, or freeze. These ancient survival strategies show up in modern financial life all the time.

- **Fight** looks like tackling money head-on—sometimes aggressively. You might micromanage every penny, argue with a partner about bills, or spend defiantly when frustrated.

- **Flight** appears as avoidance: ignoring emails from the bank, leaving bills unopened, or scrolling past reminders.

- **Freeze** is paralysis. You might want to budget but feel so overwhelmed you don't start. Even small tasks like moving money into savings can feel impossible.

Each response is your body trying to protect you from discomfort. The problem is that protection often comes at a cost—missed payments, overspending, or heightened anxiety.

Take the example of Fatima, who avoided checking her student loan balances for years. For her, it wasn't laziness; it was a stress response. Facing the numbers felt unbearable. Once she recognized that avoidance was "flight mode," she could choose a gentle first step: glancing at her balance once a week. Over time, this small practice reduced her paralysis and gave her a sense of control.

Your challenge isn't to eliminate these responses—they're part of being human. Instead, it's about noticing which one you default to and supporting yourself through it. When you catch yourself fighting, fleeing, or freezing around money, pause and ask: *What's the kindest next step I could take here?*

Retail Therapy: Why We Shop When Stressed

There's a common phrase for emotional spending: "retail therapy." And while it often gets joked about, the truth is that it works—at least temporarily. Clicking "add to cart" or swiping your card releases a burst of dopamine, the brain's reward chemical. That little hit of pleasure can feel like a breath of fresh air after a tough day.

This is why many people fall into the cycle of stress-spending. Loneliness, anger, or exhaustion can all trigger the brain to seek relief in shopping. The relief doesn't last, of course, and guilt often follows. But in the moment, the purchase eases discomfort in a way few other things do.

The problem isn't the occasional treat—it's when shopping becomes the go-to coping mechanism for emotions. A tough phone call, a stressful work deadline, or even a small conflict at home can all end in impulse purchases. Over time, money habits begin to reflect emotional patterns more than financial goals.

So what can you do?

Step One: Pause and Identify

The next time you feel the urge to shop, stop and ask yourself:

- *What am I really looking for right now—comfort, excitement, connection, distraction?*

- *Will this purchase give me that feeling, or just a quick fix?*

Sometimes simply naming the deeper need is enough to break the automatic cycle.

Step Two: Replace the Reward

Your brain is craving relief. Instead of denying it altogether, offer an alternative reward. Call a friend, go for a walk, or make a cup of tea. These may not give the same dopamine rush as buying something new, but over time they build healthier patterns of comfort.

Step Three: Build Awareness With Writing

Try this reflection: write down the last few impulse purchases you made. Next to each one, jot down the feeling you remember before buying it. Look for patterns. Did stress drive most of them? Was loneliness a common trigger? Awareness brings choice—and choice opens the door to change.

Tools for Emotional Awareness

To bring these ideas into practice, try the "Name-and-Pause" technique.

1. **Notice** the urge to spend or avoid.

2. **Name** the emotion in one word—stressed, bored, excited.

3. **Pause** by taking three slow breaths.

4. **Decide**: Ask yourself, *Does this action align with my values and goals, or is it just short-term relief?*

If you're unsure, give yourself ten minutes before acting. That space is often enough to shift from autopilot to conscious choice.

Another exercise: before making a purchase, write down, *I feel ____. I want to _____. Does this fit my goals?* You'll be surprised how much clarity this brings.

Transition

Once you begin noticing your emotions around money, you can see how they connect to habits. Stress, boredom, or anxiety don't just influence one-off decisions—they become the cues that trigger financial routines. In the next section, we'll explore the **science of habits**: how the brain hardwires money behaviors, and how you can rewire them with small, deliberate changes.

The Science of Money Habits

Think of the moment you automatically grab your phone to check your bank balance, or the routine stop for coffee on the way to work. These aren't random choices—they're habits, quietly shaping your financial life.

Habits form in the brain through what psychologists call a **loop**: a cue, a routine, and a reward. Payday hits (cue), you feel the urge to splurge (routine), and you get a burst of pleasure or relief (reward). The cycle repeats itself until it becomes second nature.

This efficiency is part of why habits are so powerful. Your brain loves shortcuts. Instead of wrestling with every decision, it runs on autopilot, saving energy for other tasks. Unfortunately, the brain doesn't distinguish between helpful habits (like setting aside savings automatically) and harmful ones (like stress-spending after a tough day). Both get wired in.

How Emotions Drive Habits

If you've ever found yourself shopping online after a frustrating meeting or avoiding your banking app after a stressful week, you've experienced how emotions fuel habit loops. The emotion itself—stress, fear, boredom—acts as the cue. The routine might be clicking "buy now" or ignoring bills. The reward? Either a dopamine hit from shopping or temporary relief from avoiding the problem.

Over time, these loops become so ingrained that changing them feels like swimming upstream. Even when you *know* better logically, your brain still prefers the familiar pattern. This is why someone can create a budget on Sunday and break it by Friday—it's not weakness; it's wiring.

Why Rewards Stick So Strongly

Every time you spend or save, your brain evaluates how it feels. That emotional evaluation is stored with the memory. A purchase that brings excitement reinforces the urge to buy again next time you're stressed. Watching a savings account grow, on the other hand, builds a quieter, steadier pride that reinforces patience.

The challenge? Immediate rewards often feel louder than long-term ones. Ordering takeout after a bad day delivers an instant dopamine spike. Watching a retirement fund grow feels satisfying too—but it unfolds over years, not seconds.

Consider two examples:

- Ana, who buys dinner impulsively after a stressful day, gets a jolt of pleasure that encourages the same behavior in the future.

- Jamal, who saves ten dollars a week, feels a subtler satisfaction that builds over months. It may not thrill in the moment, but it wires his brain for long-term security.

The key to shifting habits lies in learning to recognize which rewards truly serve you—and which simply soothe you temporarily.

Why Willpower Isn't Enough

If you've ever tried to "just stop" spending impulsively, you know how hard it is. That's because willpower alone can't erase old pathways in the brain. Those neural tracks are still there, ready to light up the moment stress or temptation hits.

Think of it like trying to stop using a well-worn road overnight. Even if you build a new path, the old one is still faster and easier—until the new road gets used often enough to become your default.

This explains why setbacks are so common. Jamie, for instance, vowed to avoid online shopping for a month. She stuck with it—until a stressful Friday sent her back to scrolling sales. Instead of seeing the slip as failure, Jamie learned to recognize it as her brain defaulting to the old route. With patience, she kept practicing her new habits until they became more automatic.

The truth is, habit change is less about perfection and more about persistence.

The Power of Micro-Habits

Big overhauls often fail because they're overwhelming. Micro-habits—tiny, consistent changes—work because they're achievable and sustainable.

A few examples:

- Rounding up each purchase and moving the spare change into savings.

- Checking your balance once a week, not every day.
- Pausing for a single deep breath before clicking "checkout."

These actions may seem too small to matter, but they create momentum. Each micro-shift builds confidence, and confidence fuels consistency. Over weeks and months, those tiny changes compound into transformation.

Try this reflective exercise: *What is one mini money habit I could start today—something so simple I can't say no?* It might be tracking just one expense, setting a $1 recurring transfer, or opening your bank app once a week. Pay attention not only to the action, but to the emotion that follows—pride, relief, curiosity. Those feelings are the seeds of stronger habits.

Reframing Setbacks

When you slip back into old routines, it's tempting to feel shame. But neuroscience reframes this: setbacks aren't proof of weakness; they're evidence of old wiring still competing with the new. Every attempt strengthens the fresh path, while each compassionate response to a slip makes it easier to keep going.

Imagine treating each setback as information rather than failure. Instead of "I blew it," the thought becomes, "Ah, stress is still my cue to shop. How else can I handle stress next time?" This shift transforms shame into curiosity—and curiosity fuels growth.

The breakthrough is realizing that change doesn't require a massive reset. It requires repetition, gentleness, and patience. The brain can—and does—rewire itself. With micro-habits, intentional rewards, and compassionate persistence, you can create financial patterns that align with your goals instead of fighting against them.

Transition

Now that we've explored how the brain creates money habits, the next step is addressing what happens when awareness and habit change still aren't enough. That's where the emerging field of **financial therapy** comes in—an approach that blends practical strategies with emotional healing to create real, lasting change.

Introducing Financial Therapy

By now you've seen how money beliefs, emotions, and habits intertwine. But sometimes, even with awareness and small changes, you still find yourself repeating the same patterns. That's because the roots of financial behavior often run deeper than logic or planning can reach. This is where **financial therapy** comes in.

Financial therapy blends the practical side of money management with the emotional insights of psychology. Unlike traditional financial advising, which focuses mainly on numbers and strategies, financial therapy asks:

- Why do I freeze when I open my banking app?
- Why do I spend impulsively when I feel lonely?
- Why does guilt follow me every time I buy something, even when I can afford it?

It's not about budgets alone. It's about understanding the hidden feelings, stories, and beliefs that shape your financial choices.

How Financial Therapy Works

Financial therapy uses a range of tools designed to bridge the gap between what you know you *should* do and what you actually *feel able* to do.

- **Journaling:** Not just writing down expenses, but also capturing the emotions tied to them. For example, noting, "Bought coffee as a reward for finishing a tough project" or "Felt anxious paying the credit card bill." Over time, this creates a map of emotional triggers and financial behaviors.

- **Guided imagery:** Visualizing yourself handling financial stress with confidence, or picturing a moment of financial peace. This rewires your brain to expect success rather than fear.

- **Conversations:** Talking openly about money—whether with a therapist, partner, or trusted friend—helps release shame and secrecy. Simply speaking aloud what you've never dared to say ("I feel embarrassed about my debt" or "I'm scared of running out") can break the silence that keeps fear in place.

Each of these practices creates a bridge between thought and feeling, giving you both clarity and compassion.

Emotional Healing Matters

Most people already know the basics: spend less than you earn, save regularly, avoid debt when possible. And yet, many still struggle. Why? Because knowledge without healing is incomplete.

Money avoidance, overspending, or staying silent in financial conflicts rarely come from ignorance. They come from deeper wounds: shame about past mistakes, pressure to look successful, or scarcity lessons carried from childhood.

Healing those emotional roots is what allows change to last. Without that step, even the best financial plan can collapse the moment stress or fear takes over.

Sometimes the real breakthrough isn't a clever budgeting trick—it's the realization: *"My money fears are old stories. I can write a new one."*

No One-Size-Fits-All

Financial therapy isn't rigid. It adapts to different cultures, backgrounds, and life stages.

- One person may need to work through cultural taboos about discussing money openly, learning to build confidence in financial conversations.

- Another may be facing job loss and use therapy to process grief and anxiety while building a new sense of security.

- Someone else may want to rewrite the perfectionism that keeps them paralyzed, unable to take even small money steps.

Your story is unique, and so is the path forward. What matters is honoring your starting point and moving at a pace that feels safe and sustainable.

Bringing It All Together

Throughout this chapter, we've uncovered the truth that money is never just math. It is shaped by your childhood lessons, cultural messages, emotional triggers, and ingrained habits. These hidden influences quietly drive decisions long before numbers hit the page.

By examining your earliest money beliefs, you begin to see where unhelpful scripts were written. By noticing your emotional responses, you gain power over moments that once felt automatic. By understanding habit loops, you learn why change is hard—and how micro-shifts make it possible. And by exploring financial therapy, you discover that healing your relationship with money requires both practical tools and emotional compassion.

The journey forward doesn't demand perfection or overnight change. It asks only for curiosity, patience, and persistence. Small pauses, mindful reflections, and gentle rewrites of old stories create the foundation for lasting financial peace.

As you move into the next chapter, keep this truth in mind: **Your money story isn't fixed.** Every belief, every habit, every emotional pattern can be understood, softened, and rewritten. The more awareness you bring to your financial life, the more freedom you gain to build one rooted in security, confidence, and ease.

Your 30-Day Money Reset

Day 1

Notice Your Money Story. Write down three memories or experiences that shaped how you feel about money. Don't edit or judge — just observe.

Chapter Two

The Messy Middle

There is a stage of change that almost no one prepares you for.

It's the part after you've decided to do things differently — but before anything looks different.

You've learned enough to know why your old patterns weren't working. You've started making quieter, more intentional choices. You're no longer operating on autopilot.

And yet, from the outside, nothing seems to have changed.

This is the messy middle.

It's the space where effort outweighs evidence. Where discipline shows up long before results. Where you're doing the work without any reliable feedback loop to tell you whether it's paying off.

Most people assume this stage means something has gone wrong.

It doesn't.

It means something important is happening beneath the surface.

When Progress Doesn't Look Like Progress

The messy middle often feels uncomfortable because it lacks the signals we're used to relying on.

There's no dramatic turnaround. No clear milestone that announces, *You're on the right track now.* Instead, there are small, almost unremarkable shifts — a pause before spending, a calmer reaction to an unexpected bill, a decision made without spiralling into guilt or panic.

These changes don't photograph well. They don't invite praise. And they rarely feel satisfying in the moment.

But they matter more than they look like they do.

Early on, most financial change is internal. It shows up in your nervous system before it shows up in your bank account. In how quickly you recover from stress. In whether you avoid or face your numbers. In whether money decisions feel charged or manageable.

That kind of progress is easy to dismiss — especially if you're used to measuring success only by visible outcomes.

This is where many people tell themselves a quiet lie:

If this were really working, I'd feel more confident by now.

But confidence is not a prerequisite for change.

It's a byproduct of repetition.

The Highlight Reel Problem

Not long ago, my son looked at what I was building and said, "It feels like you got successful really quickly."

I understood why it looked that way.

What he was seeing was the highlight reel — the visible outcome after years of invisible work.

What he hadn't seen were the ordinary days before that. The learning curve. The adjustments that didn't pay off immediately. The long stretches where I was doing the right things without any reassurance that they were enough.

That's how success usually works.

Most people only ever see about five percent of the story — the part that happens after momentum has already been built. They see the result, not the repetition. The clarity, not the confusion that came before it.

This creates a dangerous comparison trap.

When you measure your behind-the-scenes effort against someone else's front-facing outcome, it's easy to assume you're failing — when in reality, you're just earlier in the process.

The messy middle disappears from public view, but it never disappears from real life.

Every meaningful change passes through it.

Why Most People Quit Here

People rarely stop because they aren't capable.

They stop because the middle offers very little emotional reward.

In the early phase of change, motivation is high. There's relief in finally deciding to do something differently. There's energy in learning new ideas and imagining a better future.

Later, once results arrive, there's validation. Proof. A sense of arrival.

The middle has neither.

For me, this was also the stage where the absence of external support became impossible to ignore.

There were moments at home where the work I was doing barely registered. Conversations that mattered deeply to me sounded repetitive to others. At one point, my husband said, half-joking, half-weary, *"Do we really need to talk about the books again?"*

Family members didn't ask how it was going — not because they were unkind, but because they didn't understand what I was trying to build. Friends were busy with their own lives. Most had no context for the long-term vision, and even less interest in the details.

That surprised me at first. I assumed the people closest to me would be the most invested.

They weren't.

And that turned out to be an important lesson.

When you're in the messy middle, you often can't rely on encouragement from the people you love — not because they don't care about *you*, but because they don't see what you see. They don't feel the internal shifts. They don't live inside the daily repetition.

What I learned is that expecting consistent validation from those closest to you can quietly drain your momentum.

Strangely, the encouragement that mattered most often came from strangers — a message from someone who had read my work, a comment from someone who recognised themselves in a sentence, a quiet *"this helped me"* from someone I'd never met.

Those moments carried weight because they were unfiltered. They weren't shaped by shared history or emotional proximity. They were responses to the work itself.

The messy middle doesn't just test your systems.

It tests your expectations.

It asks whether you can keep going without applause — even when the people you hoped would notice don't.

What Actually Carries You Through

If motivation and confidence can't be relied on in the middle, what can?

Structure.

Simple systems that function even when you don't feel inspired. Habits that don't depend on enthusiasm. Processes that remove the need to negotiate with yourself every day.

Structure does something powerful: it reduces emotional load.

Instead of asking, *Do I feel like doing this today?* the question becomes, *What's the next small step I've already decided on?*

This is why change becomes sustainable when it's boring.

Boring means repeatable.

Repeatable means dependable.

And dependable actions are what rewire behaviour.

In the messy middle, the goal is not to feel certain. It's to stay consistent.

Every time you follow through on a small action — even when it feels insignificant — you're sending your brain a new message: *I can be trusted to show up.*

That message compounds.

Over time, it becomes self-respect. Then confidence follows.

The Middle Is an Identity Shift

One of the reasons the messy middle feels so disorienting is that it's not just about money.

It's about identity.

Your old habits were tied to an old version of you — one shaped by past experiences, emotional patterns, and learned responses. As you change your behaviour, that identity starts to loosen.

But the new identity hasn't fully formed yet.

You're no longer who you were — but you're not quite who you're becoming.

That in-between space can feel unstable.

You might find yourself thinking:

I don't react the way I used to — but I don't feel confident either.

That's not confusion.

It's transition.

This is where real change is happening.

When you stay in the middle, you allow your nervous system to recalibrate. You learn that discomfort doesn't equal danger. That uncertainty doesn't require escape. That progress can exist without applause.

That's how identity shifts — quietly, through lived experience.

Reframing the Silence

The absence of feedback doesn't mean nothing is happening.

It means the work is internal.

Think of it like building foundations below ground. No one praises concrete curing. No one celebrates wiring behind walls. But without those invisible stages, nothing above them holds.

The messy middle is structural.

It's where habits stabilise, emotions regulate, and new patterns become familiar enough to stick.

If you leave too early, you don't just abandon progress — you abandon the part that makes progress last.

Your Reset Step

Name the Middle.

Take a few minutes today to write down one area of your financial life where you're doing the work but not seeing clear results yet.

Then answer this question honestly:

What has changed internally, even if nothing looks different externally?

Look for small shifts — calmer reactions, fewer avoidance behaviours, more intentional decisions.

Those changes count.

They are evidence.

Staying in the middle isn't weakness.

It's commitment in its most honest form.

And it's where everything worth building actually takes shape.

Your 30-Day Money Reset

Day 2

Track One Emotion. Pay attention to a single emotion that arises when you deal with money today (stress, guilt, pride, relief). Jot it down when it happens.

Chapter Three

The Generational Echo — How Family Stories Shape Your Wallet

Inherited Money Scripts

Long before we open our first bank account, apply for a job, or pay a bill, our relationship with money is being written for us. The lessons come quietly—through overheard arguments, unspoken tensions, cultural traditions, and the daily choices of our caregivers. These experiences combine into what psychologists call **money scripts**: deeply ingrained beliefs that shape how we view earning, saving, spending, and sharing.

Some scripts are empowering. Others are limiting. All of them carry the fingerprints of generations before us.

Think about your own family history. Perhaps your grandparents lived through a war, rationing food and stretching every coin. Their survival mindset may have been passed to your parents, who taught you that "you can never be too careful with money." Or maybe you grew up in a family that celebrated financial success as the ultimate achievement, leaving you with the belief that your worth is measured by your income. These stories don't vanish—they echo forward, influencing choices long after the circumstances that created them have changed.

Family Lessons, Silent and Spoken

Family money lessons often come in two forms: the **spoken rules** and the **silent behaviors**.

- **Spoken rules** are the explicit lessons: "Always save for a rainy day," "Never talk about money at the dinner table," "Debt is dangerous." These messages may have been repeated so often that they feel like universal truths rather than family opinions.

- **Silent behaviors** are even more powerful. You may have never been told directly that money was stressful, but you felt the tension in the room when bills arrived. You may have watched your father hide purchases or your mother sigh with relief when paychecks cleared. These nonverbal cues often carry more weight than words.

Even generosity or secrecy can become inherited habits. A parent who grew up in poverty may give away money freely as an act of resistance—"I'll never let anyone feel the lack I felt." Another may cling to every dollar, driven by fear that scarcity will return. Children raised in these environments absorb the emotions first, then build beliefs around them.

Cultural Inheritance

Beyond family, culture also shapes our money scripts.

In some communities, wealth is seen as a collective resource, to be shared across extended family. In others, independence and individual accumulation are emphasized. In some, money is not openly discussed at all, while in others, financial transparency is seen as essential.

For example, in immigrant families, the script may revolve around sacrifice: parents working multiple jobs to provide opportunities for their children. This often leaves the next generation carrying both gratitude and pressure—the belief that they must work tirelessly to honor those sacrifices. Another cultural script might frame money as tied to status or honor, where financial achievement is equated with respectability.

Whether rooted in resilience, secrecy, pride, or shame, these cultural narratives become the soil from which personal money habits grow.

The Subtle Power of Story

One of the most striking aspects of inherited money scripts is how often they go unquestioned. When you grow up hearing, "We can't afford that," or "Money doesn't grow on trees," those statements don't feel like opinions; they feel like facts.

Over time, these repeated phrases form the invisible framework of adult decision-making. A person who grew up hearing constant warnings about debt may avoid borrowing entirely—even when a well-structured loan could help them build wealth. Another who grew up hearing "spend it while you have it" may struggle to save, even if their income is steady.

These inherited beliefs become so woven into daily life that they often feel like personality traits rather than learned behaviors. You might say,

"I'm just bad with money," without realizing you're echoing a script handed down decades before you were born.

Case Snapshot

Take Daniel, whose parents constantly reminded him that money was tight. Even after building a successful career, Daniel still feels anxious about spending. He avoids vacations, underpays himself in his own business, and double-checks every expense—even when he has more than enough. His scarcity mindset wasn't born of his reality but of his parents' fear, passed down like an heirloom.

Contrast this with Maya, who grew up watching her grandmother give money freely to neighbors in need. Maya inherited the belief that money is meant to flow, not be hoarded. As an adult, she finds joy in generosity, often donating to causes or supporting friends. While this has created deep fulfillment, it has also led to challenges when her giving outpaces her ability to save.

Neither script is inherently right or wrong. But both highlight how much our money choices are shaped by the stories of those who came before us.

Reflection Exercise

Begin exploring your own inherited money scripts with these prompts:

- What money phrases do I remember most from childhood?
- How did my parents or caregivers talk about debt, saving, or wealth?
- What feelings did I pick up—fear, pride, secrecy, shame, hope—when money was discussed (or avoided)?

- Which of those beliefs still serve me, and which might be limiting me today?

Write your answers without judgment. The goal isn't to criticize your family—it's to understand the origins of your current relationship with money.

A Bridge to What's Next

Inherited money scripts explain why many of us carry beliefs that don't match our current reality. Scarcity mindsets from grandparents who endured economic hardship can linger even when we live with relative security. Beliefs equating self-worth with income can drive us into exhaustion long after the original message has lost relevance.

Awareness is the first step. Once you begin to identify the generational echoes in your financial life, you gain the power to decide whether to keep them or rewrite them.

In the next section, we'll explore how **financial trauma from past generations**—recessions, job loss, debt, or displacement—can leave emotional scars that quietly shape your money decisions today.

The Weight of Financial Trauma

Money trauma is rarely just personal—it often runs through generations. The experiences of our parents and grandparents leave a mark that extends far beyond their lifetimes, shaping how we view financial risk, security, and success. These inherited wounds may not be visible in a bank account, but they are deeply embedded in emotions, behaviors, and attitudes toward money.

How Generational Hardship Shapes Beliefs

Imagine growing up during the Great Depression. Jobs were scarce, banks collapsed, and families often lived on the edge of survival. Children raised in that era carried forward the belief that scarcity is the default state of life. They may have become meticulous savers, distrustful of institutions, or deeply anxious about spending.

Even after times improved, many passed down this caution to their children. Their grandchildren—decades removed from the Depression—still feel the weight of that anxiety, perhaps never fully understanding where it came from.

This is how financial trauma works: once an event shakes a family's sense of security, the lessons and coping strategies developed in that moment often become permanent, influencing generations that never experienced the original hardship.

Everyday Examples of Financial Trauma

Financial trauma isn't only shaped by global events. It can stem from more personal or localized crises:

- **Job Loss or Business Failure:** If a parent lost a job suddenly, their children may grow up believing employment is always precarious. As adults, they may overwork or avoid career risks, fearing instability.

- **Debt and Bankruptcy:** Witnessing a family collapse under debt can create a lifelong aversion to borrowing—even when debt might be a tool for growth.

- **Migration and Displacement:** Families who left everything behind to start over often pass down values of frugality, sacrifice, and relentless work ethic. These can become both strengths and burdens for the next generation.

- **Addiction or Financial Abuse:** Growing up in a household where money was mismanaged—or used as a tool of control—can leave children distrustful of both others and themselves when it comes to finances.

Each of these scenarios carries not only financial consequences but also emotional weight: fear, shame, mistrust, or hyper-vigilance.

Emotional Imprints Passed Down

What makes financial trauma so enduring is the way it intertwines with emotion. A child doesn't just observe a parent losing a job—they feel the stress in the household, the arguments, the silence, the shift in mood. Those emotions become linked to money in their mind.

Later in life, they may overreact to financial stress because their nervous system associates money uncertainty with crisis. Even small setbacks—an unexpected bill, a slow month at work—can trigger a disproportionate sense of fear or failure.

Consider Sarah, who grew up with parents who constantly worried about foreclosure. Even as an adult with a steady income, she feels panic every time her mortgage payment is due. Her reality is secure, but her body still reacts to an old, inherited fear.

The Silent Burden of Shame

One of the heaviest legacies of financial trauma is shame. Families who struggled financially often internalize the belief that money problems are personal failings rather than systemic or situational challenges. That shame is rarely spoken but deeply felt.

Children absorb it without context. They might grow up believing that wanting more is greedy, or that struggling financially is a sign of weakness. This inherited shame can make it difficult to seek help, talk openly about money, or even admit to financial goals.

How Trauma Echoes in Behavior

Financial trauma often shows up in behaviors that don't match current circumstances. For example:

- Someone with plenty of savings may still clip coupons obsessively, unable to relax about spending.
- A person with stable employment may hoard cash, refusing to invest, because they fear losing everything.
- Another may overspend or give money away quickly, unconsciously reenacting the chaos they grew up with.

These behaviors can be puzzling, even to the people experiencing them. They wonder, *"Why do I worry so much when I'm objectively fine?"* The answer often lies in generational echoes.

Case Snapshot

When Jorge was a child, his father's small business collapsed, leaving the family in debt. The atmosphere at home shifted overnight—from laughter and security to tension and arguments. Jorge absorbed the message that self-employment was risky and that financial success could vanish at any moment.

As an adult, Jorge avoided entrepreneurship despite having strong business ideas. He stuck to stable, lower-paying jobs, prioritizing security over opportunity. It wasn't until he traced his avoidance back to his father's experience that he realized his fear wasn't entirely his own—it was inherited.

Reflection Exercise

Take a few moments to reflect on the history of money in your family:

- Did your parents or grandparents live through financial crises, job loss, or migration?
- How did those experiences shape the way they talked—or didn't talk—about money?
- Do you notice any echoes of those experiences in your own decisions or anxieties today?
- When you face financial stress, do you sometimes feel like your reaction is bigger than the situation warrants?

By writing these reflections down, you begin to connect the dots between your financial present and your family's financial past.

A Bridge to What's Next

Recognizing financial trauma doesn't mean blaming the generations before us. They did the best they could with what they had. The point is to notice where old fears and strategies no longer serve us.

Once you see the weight of inherited trauma, you can begin to challenge it. The next section will explore how to **break the cycle**—transforming generational money patterns so they no longer control your future.

Breaking the Cycle

Becoming aware of your inherited money scripts and financial trauma is the first step. But awareness alone isn't enough. To create meaningful change, you need to take those insights and deliberately rewrite the patterns that no longer serve you. This process is not about rejecting your family's history—it's about honoring it while choosing a different path for yourself and those who come after you.

From Unconscious Repetition to Conscious Choice

Most of us repeat our family's financial patterns without realizing it. A scarcity mindset shows up as constant worry about not having enough, even when life is stable. An overemphasis on status might push you to spend more than you can afford to keep up appearances. Avoidance habits may cause you to ignore bills, just as your parents did.

The cycle continues until you pause and ask: *Whose story am I living?*

Breaking the cycle means shifting from unconscious repetition to conscious choice. You may still decide to save diligently, spend generously, or avoid risky investments—but this time, the decision comes from your own values, not inherited fear.

Honoring the Past Without Being Controlled by It

It's important to approach this process with compassion. Many financial habits that seem limiting today were survival strategies in the past. If your grandparents clung to every penny, it was because they endured scarcity. If your parents discouraged debt, it may have been because they watched neighbors lose everything to loans.

These strategies served a purpose. Honoring that purpose allows you to release the guilt or resentment that often comes with financial inheritance. You can acknowledge, *"This made sense for them, but I don't need to carry it forward."*

Small Acts of Rebellion

Breaking generational patterns often begins with small acts of financial "rebellion." These are moments when you choose differently, even in subtle ways.

- If you grew up in a family where money was never discussed, rebellion might mean starting an open conversation with your partner about finances.
- If you inherited a scarcity mindset, rebellion might be allowing yourself a guilt-free purchase—a dinner out, a vacation, a class—without justification.
- If your family equated success with income, rebellion might mean valuing work-life balance over a higher paycheck.

These small shifts may feel uncomfortable at first, but they signal to your brain that you are creating new rules. Over time, they become powerful steps toward rewriting your story.

Reframing Limiting Beliefs

Many inherited money scripts boil down to limiting beliefs: "There's never enough," "Rich people are greedy," "Talking about money is impolite." Breaking the cycle involves questioning these beliefs and reframing them into something more supportive.

- "There's never enough" can become "I have the ability to create and manage resources."

- "Rich people are greedy" can become "Wealth can be used as a tool for good."
- "Talking about money is impolite" can become "Open conversations about money build trust and clarity."

This reframing doesn't happen overnight. It takes repetition, patience, and practice. But each time you challenge a limiting belief, you weaken its hold.

Case Snapshot

Elena grew up in a household where her parents constantly warned her not to "waste money." Every purchase came with scrutiny. As an adult, Elena found herself paralyzed when spending—even on necessities. She realized she had internalized her parents' fear.

Her turning point came when she began practicing a new belief: "Spending on essentials supports my well-being." At first, it felt unnatural. But by repeating it, journaling about it, and noticing the relief she felt when she bought healthy food or paid for reliable services, Elena gradually loosened the grip of scarcity thinking. Today, she balances saving with spending confidently, free from the fear that once controlled her choices.

Building New Family Narratives

Breaking cycles isn't just about individual healing—it also creates ripple effects for future generations. When you choose to talk openly about money with your children, you give them permission to do the same. When you model balance—saving responsibly but also enjoying life—you pass down healthier habits.

Each conversation, each intentional decision, is an opportunity to write a new family narrative. Instead of passing on anxiety or secrecy, you pass on confidence and clarity.

Reflection Exercise

Take a moment to reflect on the following prompts:

- Which of my financial habits feel like echoes of my parents or grandparents?
- What is one belief about money I inherited that I no longer agree with?
- What would it look like to gently rebel against that belief in my life today?
- If I could pass down one new money story to the next generation, what would it be?

Write freely, without worrying about "right answers." These reflections help you identify where the cycle can be broken and where new stories can begin.

A Bridge to What's Next

Breaking free from inherited patterns is an act of courage. It requires awareness, compassion, and persistence. But it's also profoundly liberating. Each small act of rebellion, each reframed belief, and each conscious decision adds up to a new financial legacy.

In the next section, we'll explore **practical tools for rewriting generational scripts**—concrete exercises, conversations, and affirmations that help solidify your new money story.

Practical Tools for Rewriting Generational Scripts

Awareness of your money story is powerful. But real transformation happens when you take that insight and apply it consistently in daily life. Rewriting generational money scripts isn't about making one dramatic change—it's about small, steady practices that gradually reshape the way you think, feel, and act around money.

Below are practical tools to help you move from recognition to rewiring. Use them as experiments, not rigid rules. Some will resonate more than others. The goal is to find practices that help you loosen the grip of old beliefs and strengthen new, empowering ones.

1. Journaling Prompts to Surface and Shift Beliefs

Writing is one of the simplest and most effective ways to bring subconscious scripts into awareness. Set aside ten minutes with a notebook and try these prompts:

- What money phrases did I hear most often as a child?
- How did those phrases make me feel at the time? How do they

affect me now?

- What money beliefs did my parents or caregivers pass on—intentionally or unintentionally?
- Which of those beliefs do I want to keep? Which do I want to release?
- What new belief would better support the life I'm building today?

Once you identify a limiting belief, write a gentle reframe. For example:

- Old script: "I must hold onto every dollar or I'll lose everything."
- New script: "I can spend on essentials and still remain safe."

Revisit these reframes daily. The repetition helps your brain begin to accept the new belief.

2. Money Conversations with Family

Silence around money often perpetuates generational patterns. Breaking the silence—whether with parents, siblings, partners, or children—can begin to shift the narrative.

Start small. You don't need to reveal your entire financial picture right away. Instead, try opening with reflection-based questions:

- "What money lessons did you grow up with?"
- "What do you think our family's biggest strength with money has been?"

- "What do you wish you had learned earlier about money?"

These conversations can be uncomfortable at first, especially if your family has avoided money talk. But often, you'll find that others share similar struggles, fears, or hopes. Talking openly helps dissolve shame and normalizes the idea that money is something to be discussed and learned, not hidden.

3. Affirmations That Anchor New Beliefs

Affirmations can feel awkward at first, but they work because they replace old narratives with intentional new ones. Try writing three money affirmations that directly challenge your inherited limiting beliefs.

Examples:

- "I am capable of creating stability, no matter my past."
- "I honor my family's sacrifices, but I choose freedom over fear."
- "Money is a tool I can use with confidence and compassion."

Repeat these aloud each morning or write them in your journal at the end of the day. Over time, they become mental counterweights to the old scripts you're trying to release.

4. Creating Rituals of Financial Empowerment

Habits stick more easily when tied to rituals. By creating small, meaningful routines, you signal to yourself that you're stepping into a new money story.

Examples include:

- Lighting a candle before reviewing your budget, turning a stressful task into a calming ritual.

- Playing uplifting music while you pay bills, reframing the act as one of empowerment.
- Setting a monthly "money date" with yourself or a partner to review goals, celebrate wins, and make adjustments.

These rituals shift money tasks from chores to conscious acts of self-care.

5. Practicing Micro-Rebellions

If your inherited scripts lean toward scarcity, over-caution, or secrecy, try small "micro-rebellions" that gently push against those patterns.

- If guilt arises when you spend, buy yourself a small treat—without explanation—and notice the feelings that surface.
- If secrecy was the norm, share one financial goal with a trusted friend.
- If your family avoided risk at all costs, take a calculated, safe step toward growth—like enrolling in a new course or starting a modest investment.

These experiments train your brain to see that breaking old rules doesn't lead to disaster. In fact, it often opens the door to freedom.

6. Visualization for Future Generations

A powerful exercise is to imagine yourself speaking directly to future generations—your children, nieces, nephews, or even your younger self. Ask:

- What money story do I want them to inherit?

- How would I explain money in a way that brings hope, not fear?
- What lesson would I want them to remember when they face a setback?

Writing a short letter or visualization around this idea not only clarifies your values but also motivates you to embody them in your own financial choices today.

Case Snapshot

David grew up hearing, "We can't afford it" nearly every day. As an adult, he earned a comfortable salary but found himself anxious about every purchase. Through journaling, David identified his core inherited belief: that money was always on the edge of disappearing.

He created a new affirmation—"My needs are met, and I have enough for today." Each time he caught himself spiraling, he repeated it. He also began a monthly ritual of reviewing his savings while enjoying his favorite coffee, reframing the act as one of security rather than stress.

Over time, David's anxiety softened. He still saved diligently, but he no longer carried the constant fear of collapse. His new money story became one of stability rather than scarcity.

Reflection Exercise

Try this today: Choose one of the tools above—journaling, conversation, affirmation, ritual, micro-rebellion, or visualization—and practice it this week. Notice what emotions surface. Does it feel freeing? Uncomfortable? Both? Write down what you experience.

Remember, the goal isn't perfection. It's progress. Each time you challenge an old script, you carve space for a healthier one to grow.

A Bridge to What's Next

Rewriting generational scripts isn't just about you. It creates ripple effects—changing the way money is discussed, felt, and experienced in your family and community.

In the final section of this chapter, we'll bring everything together—examining how inherited stories, trauma, and new tools combine to shape the financial legacy you are consciously building.

Bringing It All Together

Money doesn't exist in isolation. Every decision you make—whether to save, spend, invest, or avoid—sits on top of decades of family history, cultural influence, and emotional inheritance. By now, you've seen how money scripts form in childhood, how trauma echoes through generations, and how these hidden forces quietly shape your present reality.

The good news is this: your financial story is not fixed. While you may have inherited scripts, beliefs, and fears from those who came before you, you also hold the power to question, reshape, and rewrite them. Awareness turns what once felt inevitable into something flexible.

Honoring the Past, Choosing the Future

Breaking free from generational cycles doesn't mean dismissing the wisdom of your family. Many of the lessons passed down—frugality, resourcefulness, generosity—were born of necessity and resilience. They deserve respect. At the same time, you are not bound to repeat the exact same story.

You get to hold the paradox: honoring the sacrifices of the past while creating a new path for the future. Where your grandparents may have clung to scarcity as a survival strategy, you can choose balance. Where your parents may have carried shame around money struggles, you can choose openness. Where secrecy once thrived, you can choose conversation.

Each choice becomes a turning point in the story your family carries forward.

The Ripple Effect of Your Choices

It's easy to think of money work as personal, but it has ripple effects. When you talk openly about money with your children, you normalize conversations that might have been avoided for generations. When you challenge scarcity thinking, you model abundance for those around you. When you take small risks and grow from them, you show that resilience is possible.

These changes don't just benefit you—they shape the financial legacy of your entire family line. Every conscious decision becomes a seed planted for the next generation.

Progress, Not Perfection

One of the greatest traps in financial transformation is perfectionism—the belief that if you slip back into old patterns, you've failed. But change is rarely linear. Breaking cycles takes time. Sometimes, you'll catch yourself repeating the very behaviors you swore you'd leave behind. That's not failure; it's proof that you're human.

The difference now is awareness. When you recognize an old pattern resurfacing, you can pause, reflect, and choose differently next time. Each stumble is simply another opportunity to strengthen your new story.

Reflection Exercise

Pause here and write about the generational legacy you want to create. Ask yourself:

- What money story am I consciously choosing to pass down?
- Which beliefs from my family history will I honor and keep?
- Which ones will I gently release?
- How will my children, or the next generation, experience money differently because of the changes I make today?

This exercise grounds your progress in something larger than yourself. It reminds you that every small step matters, not just for your own peace of mind, but for the lives and stories of those who come after you.

Moving Forward

As you close this chapter, remember: the financial patterns you've inherited may be powerful, but they are not permanent. You have already begun the process of noticing, questioning, and shifting. The tools you've explored—journaling, reframing, conversations, affirmations—are not one-time exercises but lifelong practices.

Your money story is now yours to write. You may carry echoes of the past, but you are no longer defined by them. Each intentional choice moves you closer to a legacy of empowerment, stability, and ease.

In the next chapter, we'll take this work a step further by exploring how cultural and societal forces—beyond family alone—shape your financial identity. By widening the lens, you'll see not only how your personal story fits into a bigger picture, but also how to navigate external pressures with clarity and confidence.

Your 30-Day Money Reset

Day 3

Identify a Money Belief. Write down one belief you hold about money that may have roots in your family experience — for example, "Money always runs out" or "Talking about money is selfish." Ask: is this a fact, or a story passed down?

Day 4

Reframe a Negative Thought. Choose one belief from Day 3 and rewrite it in a supportive way. For example, "Money always runs out" becomes "I can create financial stability step by step."

Day 5

Money Check-In. Open your bank account or credit card statement and simply *look*. Don't analyze or judge yet. This step is about breaking old avoidance patterns and building awareness.

Chapter Four

The Psychology of Money — Inside Your Mind and Brain

When you sit down to decide whether to save, spend, or invest, your brain lights up in ways you might not expect. Different regions work together to weigh risks and rewards, but here's something striking: **losses hit the brain about twice as hard as gains do**. Losing $50 hurts far more than finding $50 feels good. That imbalance explains why a missed opportunity or financial setback can linger in your mind long after the event, shaping future choices with a sense of caution—or even dread.

Understanding this delicate balance between risk and reward opens a window into the complex dance of logic and emotion that drives your money habits. In this chapter, we'll explore how your brain responds to financial experiences, why fear and excitement pull your judgment in different directions, and how to recognize these patterns with compassion. By uncovering the psychology beneath your money decisions, you'll gain practical tools to bring more confidence, balance, and kindness to your financial life.

The Neuroscience of Financial Decisions

Picture yourself opening your bank app after a tough month or debating whether to invest in something new. You may hope your rational mind is running the show, but what actually happens inside your brain is more like a busy orchestra. Different sections play at different volumes depending on your mood, your stress level, and the stakes at hand.

Some regions are logical and deliberate; others are reactive and emotional. The interplay between them is why money decisions can feel so charged, even when the numbers on paper seem straightforward.

The Brain's Key Players

- **The Prefrontal Cortex (The Planner):** Located just behind your forehead, this is your brain's "CEO." It weighs options, imagines future outcomes, and helps you stick to long-term plans. When you compare savings accounts or sketch out a budget, your prefrontal cortex is leading the effort. But it also has the tough job of holding back impulsive urges. When your logical side whispers, "Don't buy those shoes—you don't need them," this is the part doing the heavy lifting.

- **The Amygdala (The Alarm Bell):** Deep inside your brain sit two almond-shaped structures that act as emotional sentinels. They light up when you sense threat or opportunity. That spike of anxiety you feel when looking at a credit card bill? Amygdala at work. The thrill of spotting a big discount? Same source. It reacts quickly, often before your logical brain catches up, which is why panic can lead to hasty choices—like selling investments in a downturn or splurging on a "must-have" sale item.

- **The Insula (The Pain Center):** This region monitors discomfort, both physical and emotional. Overspend on a meal you regret or realize you've blown past your budget, and the insula creates that sinking feeling in your gut. The stronger this sensation, the more likely you are to avoid similar losses in the future. Sometimes that helps you curb overspending. Other times, it creates paralysis, making you so afraid of repeating a mistake that you avoid financial action altogether.

Together, these regions explain why the experience of money is rarely neutral. Every purchase, every bill, every financial choice carries an emotional weight your brain can't help but measure.

The Battle of Emotion and Logic

Money decisions often come down to a tug-of-war between your emotional brain and your rational brain. Imagine scrolling through an online store late at night after a stressful day. You're tired, anxious, and craving relief. At that moment, the amygdala—the seat of your emotional reactions—turns up the volume, promising comfort through a purchase. Your logical prefrontal cortex tries to intervene, reminding you of your budget, but under stress, logic often takes the backseat.

Neurochemicals add fuel to this struggle. **Dopamine**, the brain's pleasure messenger, surges as you anticipate the thrill of buying something new. Meanwhile, **serotonin**, a chemical tied to mood, can either nudge you toward caution or make risks seem more appealing depending on its balance. These invisible forces explain why budgeting feels easy one day and impossible the next.

Why Losses Feel So Heavy

Our brains are wired to notice and avoid pain more than they are to pursue pleasure. This wiring shows up clearly in finances: the disappointment of losing money hits harder than the joy of gaining the same amount. This tendency, called *loss aversion*, often keeps people from investing or making bold changes, even when the odds of success are good.

From a survival standpoint, it makes sense. Our ancestors couldn't afford to treat risks lightly—a single wrong decision could cost food, shelter, or safety. But in today's world, this protective wiring can hold us back, making opportunities feel scarier than they really are.

Mental Shortcuts (Biases) That Trip Us Up

Your brain often leans on shortcuts to simplify complex decisions. These shortcuts, called *cognitive biases*, can be helpful—but they can also distort financial choices.

- **The Affect Heuristic:** When emotions color judgment, excitement about a stock or new gadget can blind you to risks.

- **Probability Neglect:** Small risks can feel overwhelming if they spark strong emotions, leading you to worry excessively about unlikely outcomes while ignoring more probable ones.

- **Status Quo Bias:** It often feels safer to do nothing than to change—even when the "safe" choice quietly costs more in the long run.

Recognizing these patterns isn't about labeling yourself "irrational." It's about understanding how your brain is trying—sometimes clumsily—to keep you safe.

The Brain's Gift: Change Is Always Possible

Here's the hopeful part: your brain is capable of change at any age. This ability, called *neuroplasticity*, means that every small, positive money habit creates new pathways. Think of it like walking a hiking trail. The first time you take the new path—pausing before clicking "buy," or setting aside $10 in savings—it feels rough and unfamiliar. But each time you repeat it, the trail becomes clearer and easier to follow.

Over time, the old, overgrown trail (impulsive spending, avoidance, panic) fades, and the new one (confidence, planning, resilience) becomes your default. This is why even the smallest shifts matter. They don't just change your budget; they change your brain.

A Gentle Pivot

Understanding how your mind and brain shape money choices isn't about making excuses—it's about building compassion for yourself. If you've ever wondered, *"Why do I do this when I know better?"* the answer often lies in the wiring between your emotional alarms and your logical planner.

But knowledge alone doesn't transform habits. It opens the door. What rewires your brain is daily practice—small, consistent actions that reinforce new pathways.

That's why, after these first three chapters of self-discovery, we'll soon shift from insight to practice. At the close of this chapter, I'll introduce you to a **30-Day Money Reset**: a step-by-step guide designed to help you retrain your financial brain, one manageable day at a time.

Self-Worth and Net Worth — How Self-Esteem Shapes Financial Choices

The way you see yourself quietly influences nearly every decision you make with money. When your sense of self-worth feels shaky, money can take on meanings far beyond its practical use. It becomes a source of comfort, validation, or sometimes even shame.

This is why someone who's had a discouraging week at work might reward themselves with a round of online shopping. It's not about the sweater, the gadget, or the dinner—it's about soothing the sting of not feeling good enough. Emotional spending often has less to do with the item purchased and more to do with the temporary relief it brings.

How Low Self-Esteem Fuels Money Patterns

Self-esteem is simply how much you value and respect yourself. When it's strong, you make decisions that align with your goals because you trust that you're worthy of stability and growth. But when self-esteem is low, money choices often drift toward self-sabotage.

Self-sabotage doesn't mean recklessness—it usually shows up in subtle, familiar ways:

- **Impulse Buying:** Spending money you didn't plan to spend, not for the item itself, but for the quick hit of validation.

- **Avoidance:** Ignoring bills, avoiding bank statements, or putting off financial planning. Beneath the surface might be the quiet belief: *"Why bother? I'll never get ahead anyway."*

- **Breaking Promises to Yourself:** Setting savings goals but abandoning them at the first temptation, then internalizing the story: *"I'm just bad with money."*

These patterns often trace back to old messages—family arguments about money, experiences of scarcity, or cultural pressures about success.

Real-Life Examples

Take Aliya, who consistently misses bill deadlines and racks up late fees. Each time, she shrugs it off with, *"I'm terrible with money."* That statement becomes both an excuse and a reinforcement of the belief that she can't change.

Or consider Marcus. As a child, he watched his parents argue about never having enough. Today, whenever he sets a savings goal, he spends the extra cash within days. The momentary relief of spending feels safer than the uncomfortable quiet of watching money sit unused in his account. Afterwards, guilt creeps in, strengthening his belief that he's destined to fail at saving.

Neither Aliya nor Marcus is "bad with money." They are replaying stories written long before they had a chance to question them.

Spotting the Link Between Self-Worth and Money

To see whether self-worth is affecting your own money habits, try this journaling exercise:

1. Write down three recent times you spent impulsively or avoided dealing with finances.

2. Next to each entry, note what you were feeling right before the decision.

3. Ask yourself: *"What did I believe about myself in that moment? Was I seeking comfort, recognition, or escape?"*

For example:

- *"After scrolling social media and seeing my friend's promotion, I bought clothes online. I felt like I was falling behind and needed to 'catch up.'"*

- *"When the credit card bill arrived, I left it unopened. I felt ashamed and believed I couldn't face it."*

Patterns emerge quickly. Many people find that repeated emotions—like not measuring up, fearing scarcity, or craving comfort—sit beneath their financial behaviors.

Breaking the Cycle of Self-Sabotage

Healing begins when you gently challenge the idea that your financial mistakes define your worth. Your value as a person is not tied to your income, savings account, or financial "success."

Start small:

- **Daily Self-Appreciation:** Each morning, list three non-material qualities you admire about yourself. It might be your creativity, perseverance, or kindness. Anchoring your value in who you are—not what you own—gradually shifts the foundation of your self-esteem.

- **Practice Self-Compassion:** After a setback, speak to yourself the way you would to a friend. Instead of, *"I blew it again,"* try, *"I made a mistake, but I'm learning. Tomorrow is another chance."*

- **Reach for Support:** Whether it's a trusted friend, partner, or therapist, speaking openly about your struggles dissolves shame. Naming your challenges aloud robs them of their hidden power.

Affirmation Rituals

Affirmations may feel awkward at first, but they are powerful tools for reshaping inner beliefs. Choose one statement that speaks to you, such as:

- "I am worthy of financial security and peace."
- "My value is not defined by my bank balance."
- "I can learn and grow at my own pace."

Say it each morning while looking in the mirror. If resistance surfaces—thoughts like *"This isn't true"*—that's normal. It simply means the old script is strong. With repetition, the new belief begins to feel more natural.

For extra reinforcement, journal briefly after saying the affirmation: *"What emotions came up? What small action today would align with this belief?"* Over time, this practice chips away at the link between self-worth and net worth.

From Self-Worth to Relationships

As you strengthen self-worth, you may notice ripple effects in your relationships. You begin to set clearer boundaries, speak more honestly about money, and make choices that align with your values instead of old fears. This growth lays a powerful foundation for understanding how your *attachment style*—the way you connect with others emotionally—shapes money management in couples, families, and partnerships.

Recognizing this connection prepares you for the next section, where we'll explore how different attachment styles—secure, anxious, avoidant, and disorganized—show up in everyday financial decisions.

Attachment Styles Meet Money Management

Money conversations in relationships often run deeper than numbers. They touch on trust, security, and how much partners feel seen and supported. To understand why some couples handle money with ease while others fall into cycles of avoidance or conflict, it helps to look through the lens of **attachment theory**.

Attachment theory describes the emotional patterns we develop in close relationships, usually based on early life experiences. These patterns often follow us into adulthood, quietly shaping how we connect, communicate, and cope under stress. There are four main attachment styles:

- **Secure:** Comfortable with intimacy and independence, open to communication, and able to trust themselves and others.

- **Anxious:** Fearful of rejection or abandonment, seeking frequent reassurance and closeness.

- **Avoidant:** Highly value independence, may withdraw from vulnerability, and often keep details (including financial ones) private.

- **Disorganized:** A less common style combining both anxious and avoidant traits, often marked by confusion or unpredictability.

How Attachment Styles Shape Money Conversations

When two people sit down to budget, save, or spend together, their attachment patterns show up—sometimes subtly, sometimes dramatically.

- A **secure partner** feels comfortable being open about financial worries, asking questions, and making joint plans. They approach money as a shared problem to solve.

- An **anxious partner** may check balances multiple times a day, ask for frequent updates, or worry that a lack of transparency signals rejection.

- An **avoidant partner** may prefer separate bank accounts, resist joint planning, or dodge regular money talks. For them, financial independence feels safer than sharing.

- A **disorganized partner** might oscillate—overspending impulsively when they feel ignored, then withdrawing completely when conflict arises.

The numbers matter, but the real tension usually lives underneath: in fears of being controlled, abandoned, or misunderstood.

Everyday Examples

Take vacation planning. A secure couple may sit down, talk through costs, and decide together. An anxious partner, however, might secretly worry that raising concerns about money will cause rejection, so they stay silent but overspend later to "make up for it." An avoidant partner might quietly stash extra money aside "just in case," feeling uneasy about shared accounts but unwilling to say so.

Over time, these small mismatches can create a push-pull dynamic: one partner seeks connection through spending and sharing, while the other seeks safety through privacy or withdrawal. Both are trying to feel secure, but their methods clash.

Case Snapshot: Alex and Jamie

Alex and Jamie live together and share bills. Alex is an avoidant saver—organized, spreadsheet-driven, and comforted by having money tucked away in a private account. Jamie, on the other hand, is an anxious spender. When feeling distant or insecure, Jamie tends to buy small things impulsively, looking for a sense of comfort or validation.

When Alex discovers receipts for Jamie's surprise purchases, frustration bubbles up: *"Did you really need this?"* Jamie, hurt by the criticism, defends the spending: *"It was just a few things! You never tell me what you're doing with your money either."* Both retreat, feeling unseen.

On the surface, they're arguing about numbers. But beneath the surface, Alex fears being controlled, while Jamie fears being abandoned. Their money conflicts aren't flaws in character—they are reflections of attachment needs seeking safety.

From Blame to Curiosity

Healing begins when couples shift from blame to curiosity. Instead of accusing or defending, they pause to ask: *"What's really going on here?"*

A few simple practices can help:

1. **Regular Money Check-Ins:** Short, structured conversations about finances, held in a safe and calm space. Ground rules help: no shaming, no interrupting, and each person gets equal time to

share.

2. **Journaling Together:** Partners can write down their earliest money memories and current money values, then share. This fosters empathy: *"Now I understand why you want a buffer account—it makes you feel secure, not secretive."*

3. **Naming the Emotional Layer:** Instead of saying, *"You're irresponsible,"* reframe as, *"When I see surprise purchases, I feel anxious because stability is important to me."* This moves the conversation from attack to vulnerability.

4. **Celebrating Wins:** Couples often dwell on conflicts but overlook successes. Pausing to celebrate paying off a bill, reaching a savings milestone, or even just sticking to a budget meeting builds trust.

Reflection Exercise

If you're in a relationship, try this exercise with your partner:

- Each of you writes down your top three money values (e.g., security, freedom, generosity, enjoyment).
- Share them and notice where they overlap or differ.
- Then, discuss how those values connect to your earliest money memories.

This exercise shifts the conversation from "you're wrong" to "here's what shaped me." Understanding each other's histories creates compassion where there was once judgment.

Why Attachment Awareness Matters

Knowing your own attachment style doesn't just help in relationships—it also helps you navigate solo financial decisions.

- If you're anxious, you may tend to overspend when lonely or seek reassurance through shopping. Awareness allows you to pause and ask: *"What do I really need right now—comfort, or this item?"*

- If you're avoidant, you might delay seeking financial advice or keep money matters private, even when collaboration would help. Awareness lets you consider, *"What would it look like to share just one piece of my financial picture with someone I trust?"*

- If you're secure, you may find yourself naturally modeling healthy conversations for those around you. Awareness helps you extend that strength with even greater empathy.

A Foundation for the Future

Attachment patterns don't have to define you forever. They are starting points, not destinies. With awareness, communication, and consistent practice, couples and individuals can build healthier, more secure approaches to money.

This awareness also prepares you for bigger transitions—career changes, family shifts, or unexpected crises. When you understand both your own attachment style and your partner's, you're better equipped to weather those storms as a team rather than slipping back into old defensive habits.

Closing Thought

At its core, attachment awareness is about seeing money conflicts not as failures, but as opportunities to understand each other more deeply. Each small act of honesty, kindness, and curiosity builds trust—not just in your partner, but in yourself.

When emotional safety and financial stability go hand in hand, relationships become stronger, calmer, and more resilient. And whether you share finances with a partner or manage them alone, knowing how your attachment style influences your choices gives you another layer of self-awareness on the path to financial confidence.

In the next section, we'll turn from relationships outward to the inner storm many people face alone: **financial anxiety**—the worry beast that steals sleep and peace of mind.

Financial Anxiety: Taming the Worry Beast

For many people, money worry is a quiet companion that never quite goes away. It shows up as racing thoughts at bedtime, a knot in the stomach when opening bills, or a spike of dread when discussing finances with loved ones. These sensations—restlessness, irritability, sleepless nights—aren't quirks or failings. They're the body's alarm system, signaling that money stress deserves attention and care.

Think of the last time you avoided checking your bank account or felt guilt after a small splurge. Those moments are not unusual. They're shared experiences in today's world, where economic pressures, social comparisons, and unexpected expenses constantly stir anxiety.

When Concern Turns into Anxiety

Not all worry is harmful. A healthy level of caution keeps you alert, helping you save for a rainy day or double-check a budget. But when caution spirals into rumination—obsessively replaying "what if" scenarios—it crosses into financial anxiety.

Financial anxiety may look like:

- Checking your bank balance compulsively, even when nothing has changed.
- Avoiding statements or bills for weeks because facing them feels unbearable.
- Arguing over tiny purchases that symbolize bigger fears.
- Losing sleep over possible crises, even if they haven't happened.

The triggers vary. For some, it's unstable income. For others, it's debt, student loans, family obligations, or caring for aging parents. The script is the same: worry, shame, fear.

Why Money Feels Like Survival

Your body doesn't distinguish between physical danger and financial danger. When you perceive a threat to your security—whether it's a looming bill or the thought of losing a job—the fight-or-flight response kicks in. Adrenaline surges, the heart races, muscles tighten, and clear thinking vanishes.

This ancient system was designed for short bursts of danger—escaping predators, not enduring decades of bills and headlines. Chronic financial stress keeps you stuck in a loop of hyper-vigilance, where even small problems feel overwhelming. Decision-making becomes harder. Focus slips. Avoidance grows.

This explains why people often say, *"I just can't deal with it right now,"* even when ignoring finances makes the problem worse. It isn't laziness—it's biology.

Calming the Nervous System

Breaking the loop begins with calming the body. A simple grounding exercise can interrupt panic and create space for clearer choices.

Try this:

1. Sit with your feet flat on the floor.

2. Breathe in through your nose for a count of four.

3. Hold for two.

4. Exhale slowly through your mouth for six.

5. Repeat three times.

Notice your shoulders dropping, your heartbeat slowing, the air moving in and out. This practice sends your body the signal: *I am safe right now.*

Using this "reset breath" before checking your balance, paying a bill, or discussing money helps retrain your nervous system. Over time, your brain begins to associate financial tasks with calm rather than panic.

Gentle First Steps Toward Clarity

Once your body feels steadier, practical steps become possible. Think small, not sweeping.

- **Create a Simple Budget:** Not as punishment, but as clarity.

Write down essentials first—housing, food, utilities. Then add what you can toward savings or debt. Even the act of writing it down eases mental clutter.

- **Shrink the Goals:** Instead of "I'll save $10,000," start with "I'll save $5 a week." Small wins build momentum and chip away at fear.

- **Tackle One Bill at a Time:** If debt feels overwhelming, focus on a single payment. Each checkmark builds confidence.

- **Use Technology Wisely:** Apps and reminders can turn chaos into order—but only if they reduce stress. If constant alerts fuel anxiety, silence them and schedule one calm check-in per week instead.

The goal isn't perfection. It's progress. Every small action interrupts the cycle of avoidance.

Finding Safe Support

Financial anxiety thrives in silence. The more you avoid talking about it, the heavier it feels.

Consider reaching out for support in a way that feels safe:

- Share your worries with a trusted friend who listens without judgment.

- Join an online community that celebrates small wins and progress over perfection.

- Work with a financial counselor or coach who understands both the numbers and the emotions behind them.

Reaching out doesn't mean weakness—it's wisdom. Anxiety loses its grip when spoken aloud.

Stories of Change

- **The Freelancer:** A young freelancer with irregular income constantly felt behind. Instead of tracking every dollar (which triggered panic), she shifted to tracking only monthly averages. That single change reduced daily anxiety and helped her plan realistically.

- **The Parent:** A Gen X parent struggling with secrecy around bills started weekly "money check-ins" with their partner. At first, the talks felt awkward, but over time they replaced shame with teamwork.

- **The Family:** An immigrant family pooled resources into a community fund. Each milestone—a paid bill, a growing reserve—became a celebration, strengthening connection as well as financial resilience.

Each of these examples shows that while triggers differ, the path out of anxiety follows the same principles: calm the body, shrink the steps, build support.

Reflection Exercise

Pause for a few minutes and write:

- What money tasks do I avoid the most?

- What feelings rise in my body when I think about them?

- What is one gentle step I could take this week to bring clarity instead of avoidance?

This exercise is not about fixing everything at once. It's about naming your patterns with compassion and choosing a single point of movement.

Looking Ahead

Managing financial anxiety isn't about never worrying again—it's about learning to calm the body, take small actions, and reframe setbacks as learning moments. Each time you do, you weaken the old association between money and fear.

This awareness lays the groundwork for what comes next in this book. Because while understanding your brain, your self-worth, your relationships, and your anxiety is powerful, knowledge alone won't rewire habits. What changes the brain is daily practice.

That's why, as we close this chapter, we'll begin transitioning into a practical, structured program: **The 30-Day Money Reset.** This reset isn't about rules or deprivation. It's about gently retraining your brain and body with small daily steps—building new habits that stick, and creating a sense of calm confidence around money that lasts.

Your 30-Day Money Reset

Day 6

Define Security for Yourself. In your journal, write down what "financial security" personally means to you. It might be having $500 in savings, paying bills on time, or simply feeling calm when you check your accounts.

Day 7

Write a Money Intention. Capture in one sentence how you want to feel about money by the end of this Reset. For example: *"I want to feel calm and confident when I manage my money."*

Chapter Five

Your Financial Inventory — Where Are You Now?

Imagine yourself at the kitchen table, papers spread out before you—unopened bills, bank statements, maybe a few crumpled receipts pulled from a bag. The weight you feel in this moment is heavier than the paper itself. It's the build-up of months, maybe years, of putting this off. Anxiety, shame, and uncertainty swirl together, whispering reasons to walk away.

And yet, here you are.

This moment, though uncomfortable, is also a turning point. Looking directly at your finances—even if it feels daunting—is the first real step toward reclaiming control. Think of it as shining a gentle light into a dark corner. You're not here to scold or punish yourself. You're here to notice, to understand, to gather information. Numbers on a page are not a reflection of your worth. They are simply data, clues to help you write the next chapter of your money story.

This chapter will guide you through that process with warmth and clarity. Instead of rushing or criticizing, we'll slow down. You'll gather the pieces of your financial life, hold space for the feelings that surface, and begin to see a picture that makes sense. What feels like chaos now can become clarity—with kindness as your starting point.

Understanding Your Financial Inventory with Compassion

Sitting down with your finances is an act of self-care. It's not a test of how responsible you are. It's not a scorecard for your life. Many people avoid this process because of the emotions that come with it—shame about debt, guilt over past choices, or fear of what they'll find. These feelings are normal. They don't mean you're "bad with money." They simply mean you're human.

Try reframing this exercise: you are not judging yourself; you are gathering information. Each number you see is neutral until you give it meaning. Looking at a bill, a balance, or a statement is not about passing or failing—it's about starting fresh.

To make the process gentler, set up your environment with intention. Choose a quiet time when you won't be interrupted. Sit somewhere comfortable. Pour a cup of tea, light a candle, or play music that calms you. Small rituals like these send a message to your brain: *this is not punishment, this is care.*

Now, begin gathering the puzzle pieces. Collect unpaid bills, bank and credit card statements, loan documents, pay stubs, and investment account summaries. If you use budgeting apps, download the latest reports. If most of your money life lives online, write down your logins on a sticky note and keep them handy. Don't forget the little things—an old receipt from a grocery run can tell you just as much about your habits as a line item in a spreadsheet.

Expect emotions to rise as you gather. Anxiety, frustration, denial, even numbness—it's all common. These are not signs you're failing.

They are your body's way of protecting you. Notice them. Name them. If your chest tightens or your breath speeds up, pause. Step outside for a moment. Write a few lines in a journal: *"I feel anxious opening this statement, but I'm here, and I can do this."* Even three deep breaths can help reset your nervous system before you continue.

Every document you collect is progress. Every download or envelope opened is a win. Acknowledge those small victories: *"I showed up. I faced this."* Shred outdated paperwork. Organize files neatly. Celebrate the positives you find—an automatic savings transfer you forgot about, a lower balance than expected, even the simple relief of knowing exactly what's there.

And when shame or harsh inner voices rise, remember what you learned earlier about money stories. Many of those judgments aren't even yours—they were handed down from parents, culture, or past experiences. They may whisper, *"You're irresponsible,"* or *"You'll never get it right."* But they are old scripts, not truths. You have the choice to respond differently now—with self-empathy instead of criticism.

By the end of this step, you'll have more than a pile of papers—you'll have a foundation. A compassionate, honest snapshot of where you stand today. And that clarity will make every step forward lighter and easier.

Assessing Cash Flow, Savings & Debt

Now that you've gathered the pieces of your financial life, it's time to start making sense of them. Think of this as assembling a puzzle. Each statement, bill, or receipt is just one piece of the picture. When they're scattered, it feels overwhelming. But once you put them together, you begin to see where you really stand.

The key here is to approach the process gently. You're not grading yourself. You're simply noticing what's true right now, without judgment.

Tracking Your Money

The first tool in your kit is choosing a way to track your money. Some people love digital apps that do most of the heavy lifting—programs like YNAB, PocketGuard, or Empower can automatically pull in transactions, categorize spending, and give you a snapshot of your net worth. They can even flag subscriptions you've forgotten about or highlight areas where your money leaks out without you noticing.

Others prefer the tactile approach—writing things down in a spreadsheet or even a simple notebook. While it may take longer, this hands-on method often builds trust in the numbers because you're directly engaging with them. Many people find the act of writing down each expense slows them down and brings clarity.

Neither approach is "better." What matters most is consistency. Choose a method that feels comfortable and sustainable for you. Then, carve out a regular time—maybe Sunday afternoon with a warm drink, or a quiet half-hour after work—to review your money. Turning it into a ritual makes it less of a chore and more of an act of self-care.

As you track, add a simple reflection: *"What did I feel as I entered this?"* For example: *"Relief when I saw my grocery bill was lower than last month"* or *"Anxiety when I added in my credit card charge."* These notes help you see not just the numbers, but also the emotions driving your choices.

Mapping Income

Next, list every source of income that flows into your life. Go beyond your main paycheck. Include side hustles, freelance projects, rental income, government assistance, child support, or even irregular payments like annual bonuses or tax refunds.

If you live with roommates, partners, or family who share expenses, note their contributions too. Non-cash supports—like a parent covering phone bills or a friend helping with childcare—also shape your financial reality, so include them.

When you see it all in one place, it becomes easier to notice patterns. Maybe your income feels steady and secure, or maybe it's patchy and unpredictable. Either way, this snapshot helps you plan from reality instead of guesswork.

Ask yourself: *"Did any source surprise me? Do I feel relief seeing this on paper, or does it stir anxiety?"* Even discomfort is useful—it's information you can work with.

Debt Snapshot

Once you've mapped income, it's time to face debts. This can be one of the hardest steps emotionally, so remember: numbers are not judgments. They're just information.

Make a list of all your debts. For each one, include:

- The lender or creditor
- Current balance
- Interest rate
- Minimum monthly payment

Divide them into categories:

- **Secured debts** (like mortgages or car loans) are tied to assets.

- **Unsecured debts** (like credit cards or medical bills) usually carry higher interest but aren't attached to property.

When you lay this out, you may notice some debts cost you more than others. For instance, a credit card with 20% interest eats up far more energy than a low-interest student loan. This list isn't here to shame you—it's here to give you clarity.

Pause and check in with yourself: *"How does it feel to see this all at once?"* You may feel dread, relief, or both. Acknowledge it. Remind yourself: you're not failing—you're mapping.

Some people find it helpful to color-code or highlight debts that need the most urgent attention. Visual cues like this can make the repayment journey feel less overwhelming and more like a game plan.

Building Savings

Finally, let's talk about savings. Savings isn't about huge amounts—it's about steady habits. Even $5 set aside regularly makes a difference, not just in your account but in your mindset.

One of the easiest ways to grow savings is automation. Set up a recurring transfer from your checking to your savings account, schedule a payroll deduction, or use round-up features that tuck away spare change each time you spend. The goal is to make saving so easy it happens without effort.

Celebrate the first transfer, no matter how small. Acknowledge it as a win. You've proven to yourself that saving is possible. Then check in: *"Did this feel freeing? Or did I worry about cash flow?"* If it feels too tight, adjust the amount. Flexibility is key. The point isn't perfection—it's consistency.

Pulling It Together

Tracking, income mapping, debt snapshots, and savings habits are like four corners of your financial picture. Together, they transform vague stress into clear information. With practice, these steps can shift your perspective: numbers that once felt heavy and shameful become guides you can trust.

And when setbacks happen—as they inevitably will—you'll have a process to return to. Each review is not a measure of worth but an act of care. Each note you take, each habit you repeat, builds confidence over time.

The Financial Wheel of Life Exercise

True financial wellness is about more than bills, budgets, or balances. It's about how all the parts of your money life work together—saving, spending, giving, planning, enjoying. Numbers tell only part of the story; how you feel in each area fills in the rest.

The **Financial Wheel of Life** is a tool to help you see that bigger picture. It's a simple exercise that reveals where things feel balanced and where they feel out of sync. Think of it as a snapshot of your financial well-being today—without judgment, without a scorecard.

The Eight Slices of Your Wheel

Imagine a circle divided into eight equal wedges. Each wedge represents a different area of your financial life:

1. **Saving** – building a cushion for emergencies or future needs.

2. **Spending** – the day-to-day flow of money for bills, groceries, and pleasures.

3. **Debt Management** – how you handle balances, payments, and interest.

4. **Investing** – putting money to work for future growth and security.

5. **Giving** – sharing with others or supporting causes that matter to you.

6. **Earning** – the inflow of money from work, side gigs, or other sources.

7. **Planning** – budgeting, setting goals, and shaping a long-term vision.

8. **Enjoyment** – allowing yourself to experience joy and fulfillment with money.

Each slice tells part of your story. Maybe you're confident with saving but struggle with debt. Or maybe generosity comes naturally, but planning feels stressful. There's no "perfect" wheel—just an honest reflection of where you are today.

How to Create Your Wheel

1. Take a blank sheet of paper and draw a large circle.

2. Divide it into eight wedges (like a pie chart) and label each section with the categories above.

3. For each category, rate your current level of satisfaction on a

scale of 1–10. A 1 means "very dissatisfied," while 10 means "completely satisfied." Base your scores on feelings, not perfection.

Once you've scored each area, connect the dots around the wheel. You'll see a shape emerge. Is it smooth and balanced, or lopsided with dips and gaps? That shape is your personal money map.

Reflection and Awareness

Numbers on the wheel are important, but your **feelings** behind the numbers matter more.

Take a moment to write a few notes next to each category:

- What influenced your score?
- Did a recent debt payment lower your sense of peace?
- Does generosity raise your sense of joy?
- Does planning feel like a burden or a relief?

These notes help connect emotions to numbers. You may notice that high scores bring gratitude and low scores stir anxiety or frustration. This is not failure—it's feedback.

A Real-Life Example

Zoe, a busy professional, rated herself highly in **earning** and **giving** but low in **planning** and **investing**. When she reflected, she realized her generosity sometimes left her short on resources for her own dreams. Her "aha moment" was recognizing that even small changes—like scheduling a monthly money check-in or setting up an automatic transfer to investments—could bring her wheel into better balance.

Your wheel will look different. The power lies in noticing the patterns, not in comparing them to anyone else's.

Choosing Your Focus

Once your wheel is complete, choose **one area** to focus on. Start with the lowest score or the category that carries the heaviest emotional weight.

For example:

- If **savings** scored low, commit to automating just $5 a week.
- If **debt** feels heavy, make one extra payment this month.
- If **enjoyment** scored lowest, plan a small, intentional treat to remind yourself money is also for joy.

The goal isn't to "fix" the entire wheel at once—it's to take one small step that creates momentum. Over time, small changes ripple outward, and your wheel slowly smooths itself into balance.

A Gentle Reminder

The Wheel of Life isn't about creating a perfect circle. It's about insight. It's about noticing where money feels nourishing and where it drains you, so you can move forward with clarity. Each line you draw, each note you jot down, is proof that you're willing to look honestly at your financial life—and that honesty is the very foundation of change.

Emotional Check-In: Bridging Feeling and Finance

Strong emotions often rise when we sit down with our financial reality. A racing heart when opening a bill, a tight stomach while logging into online banking, even a spark of pride when spotting progress—all of these reactions are completely normal. They are signals, not verdicts. They point toward what matters to you, where you feel vulnerable, and where growth is waiting.

This part of the journey is about pausing long enough to notice those feelings, rather than pushing them aside. By checking in with your emotions as you review your finances, you bridge the gap between numbers and self-awareness—turning what could be a draining task into an opportunity for healing and clarity.

Journaling: Making Space for Your Feelings

Journaling is one of the most powerful tools for emotional clarity. It gives your feelings a safe outlet, moving them from the swirl inside your head onto the page where you can see them with fresh eyes.

Set aside 10–15 minutes in a quiet space. Don't worry about grammar or structure—just write freely. Try prompts like:

- *"What do I feel when I look at my bank statement?"*
- *"Where in my body do I notice tension when I think about debt or savings?"*
- *"When have I felt proud of a financial choice, no matter how small?"*

For example, you might write: *"Today, reviewing my credit card balance, I felt a wave of embarrassment—but also relief that I'm finally facing it."*

Your journal doesn't judge. It simply reflects back your truth, helping you see patterns and progress over time.

Naming Your Emotions

One of the simplest, yet most powerful, ways to ease financial stress is to name emotions precisely. Instead of labeling everything as "stress," try getting specific:

- *"I feel dread about a late payment."*
- *"I feel hope seeing my savings inch upward."*
- *"I feel guilt about overspending, but determination to change."*

Naming emotions brings them down to size. A vague sense of overwhelm becomes a clear, manageable feeling. Even pride, joy, or surprise deserve to be named—they remind you that money is not only a source of stress but also of empowerment and possibility.

A Mind-Body Scan

Our bodies often register money stress before our minds catch up. You might clench your jaw reading a bill, or feel a knot in your stomach while thinking about overdue debt. These signals are invitations to pause.

Try a simple scan: Sit comfortably with your feet flat on the floor. Close your eyes or soften your gaze. Slowly bring your attention from the top of your head down to your toes. Notice where tension lives—maybe your shoulders, chest, or stomach—and breathe into that space. A few slow, conscious breaths can shift your body from "fight-or-flight" into calm awareness.

If it feels overwhelming, anchor yourself by pressing your feet firmly into the floor and reminding yourself: *"I am safe in this moment."* Even two minutes of this can help emotions move through instead of sticking.

Practicing Kinder Self-Talk

Many of us carry old stories that whisper shame into our financial lives: *"I'm just bad with money."* *"I'll never get ahead."* These scripts often come from family or cultural messages, not from truth.

When emotions rise, try speaking to yourself as you would to a dear friend:

- *"It makes sense I feel anxious—this is hard, and I'm learning."*
- *"My feelings don't define me; they are experiences that will pass."*
- *"I am allowed to make mistakes and still move forward."*

Compassionate self-talk doesn't erase challenges, but it makes space for resilience. With every gentle phrase, you strengthen your ability to keep showing up without judgment.

Why This Matters

Each emotional check-in is more than a "soft" exercise—it's a building block for lasting change. Numbers without feelings can leave us cold and detached. Feelings without numbers can leave us lost and reactive. But when the two come together—practical clarity paired with emotional honesty—you gain not only insight but also the power to act with confidence.

By weaving emotions into your financial inventory, you build a new habit: one of curiosity, compassion, and courage. And that habit is just as valuable as any budget, spreadsheet, or savings account.

Reflection

Facing your finances can feel risky, messy, and uncomfortable—but by approaching each statement, receipt, and login screen with **curiosity instead of criticism**, you've already taken a courageous step. This chapter wasn't about scoring yourself or "fixing" everything at once. It was about creating a safe space to look honestly at where you are now.

Every action you took here matters: gathering documents, jotting down feelings, drawing your Wheel of Life, even pausing to breathe through a wave of anxiety. These are not small tasks. They are proof that you're willing to show up for yourself, even when it's hard.

Remember, **your financial inventory is not a judgment—it's a mirror.** It reflects both the practical numbers and the emotions that come with them. By treating what you see with compassion, you've laid the foundation for real change.

There will be setbacks. Some weeks you may feel like you're sliding backwards, or like avoidance sneaks in again. That doesn't mean you've failed. It means you're human. Progress in money, as in life, is built not on perfection but on persistence, patience, and kindness toward yourself.

As you move forward, carry this truth: clarity comes slowly, through small, repeatable acts of care. Each time you sit down with your numbers, breathe through discomfort, or write down one honest feeling, you are rewriting old stories. You are building trust with yourself.

This compassionate clarity will guide the next part of your journey—learning how to turn the numbers in front of you into a **practical, flexible system you can live with.** In Chapter 5, we'll explore how to create cash flow awareness—the gentle art of making your money visible day by day, without shame.

Your 30-Day Money Reset

Day 8

List What You Own. Write down your current assets — savings accounts, cash, retirement funds, property, or anything else of value. Don't worry about size; this is about clarity.

Day 9

List What You Owe. Write down your debts — credit cards, loans, or money borrowed. Include balances and interest rates if you can, but don't stress if you only have rough estimates.

Day 10

Create a Snapshot. Combine Days 8 and 9 into a simple one-page snapshot of your finances. This isn't about judgment — it's about seeing the full picture so you know your true starting point.

Chapter Six

The Financial Therapy Toolkit — Exercises for Change

If you've ever wondered why you keep falling into the same money patterns—overspending when stressed, avoiding bills until the last minute, or buying things for comfort you later regret—you're not alone. These habits aren't about weakness or laziness. They're often shaped by hidden stories and emotions you haven't yet had the chance to notice.

This chapter is about bringing those patterns into the light with simple, practical exercises. We'll use tools like journaling, visualization, mindfulness, and affirmations—not as abstract "self-help tricks," but as ways to gently uncover your money triggers and rewrite the old scripts that no longer serve you.

The goal isn't quick fixes. It's learning to meet your financial life with more curiosity, compassion, and clarity—so you can create lasting change that actually feels doable.

Journaling as Your First Step Toward Financial Self-Awareness

Money stress rarely shows up as just numbers. It's often wrapped in old stories, fleeting emotions, and everyday triggers. Maybe you've felt a knot in your stomach before checking your bank balance, or guilt after an impulsive online purchase. A busy parent might worry every time groceries pile up at the checkout. A freelancer might panic at the sight of irregular income. Even deciding whether to say yes to a coffee invite can stir doubt when money feels tight. These moments aren't about math—they're about emotion.

At the heart of it, money habits often repeat because they're fueled by unspoken feelings and past experiences. Maybe every stressful day at work ends with comfort takeout. Or you put off opening bills because of the dread they spark. Recognizing these "aha moments" isn't a failure—it's insight. And the first step out of autopilot is noticing, not fixing. That's where journaling becomes powerful.

Journaling slows down automatic habits and gives you a compassionate mirror. You don't need to be a writer or have long stretches of time. Just a few notes a day can help reveal what's really happening underneath your choices. If thoughts like "I should know better" come up, meet them with kindness. This process isn't about shaming yourself—it's about learning.

One of the best places to begin is the **Daily Money Diary**. For one week, record every expense—large or small—and add a note about how you felt before, during, or after spending. It can be as simple as:

- *"Coffee—$4. Rushed before, satisfied after."*
- *"Paid phone bill—relief, but also stress about next month."*

Some days, emotions will be clear. Other times, you may feel numb or on autopilot. Every entry counts, because together they show the story behind your numbers. You may discover that paying bills brings the same relief as buying a treat, or that certain times of day trigger more spending. There is no wrong way to feel—each note deepens awareness.

How to try the Daily Money Diary:

1. Choose a format—a notebook, planner, or simple digital document.
2. At the end of each day, list every purchase and the amount.
3. Add one word or phrase to capture the emotion: anxious, calm, guilty, relieved, hurried, hopeful.
4. Repeat daily for a week (missing a day or two is okay—consistency matters more than perfection).
5. Include non-purchases too, like checking your balance or declining an outing because of cost.

As you get more comfortable, expand into **Trigger Tracking**. This means noticing what happens right *before* a financial decision. Did a stressful meeting lead to late-night shopping? Did a friend's text spark dinner out? Or maybe loneliness nudged you toward buying something online. Jotting down brief notes like *"Scrolled Instagram, felt left out, bought headphones"* turns invisible patterns into visible ones. Instead of judgment, you're gathering clues about what your emotions really need.

At the end of the week, pause for a **Reflective Review**. Flip through your entries and highlight patterns. Maybe Mondays bring more stress-buys, or Fridays spark relief spending. Notice repeated emotions: does anxiety show up most often? Pride? Guilt? Then ask gentle questions:

- *When did I feel most at ease with money?*
- *Which emotions pushed me toward avoidance or impulse?*
- *Where was I proud or surprised?*

This isn't about scoring yourself. It's about shining light on hidden loops so you can meet them with compassion. Every word you write is progress.

Visualization & Guided Imagery

Awareness through journaling shows you where your emotions and money choices connect. But sometimes, even when you *understand* your patterns, the feelings still linger—anxiety before opening a bill, shame over past mistakes, or panic when unexpected expenses arise. This is where visualization and guided imagery can help. By rehearsing calm, supportive outcomes in your mind, you train both your brain and body to respond with more confidence and less fear.

Visualization is powerful because your brain responds to imagined experiences almost as if they were real. Athletes use it to prepare for competitions, and therapists use it to reduce anxiety. When applied to money, it can ease stress, reframe old stories, and help you imagine a different relationship with your finances.

Safe Place Visualization

This exercise creates an inner refuge you can return to anytime money stress spikes.

1. Sit comfortably in a quiet space.

2. Close your eyes and imagine a place where you feel completely

safe. It might be a real location, like a favorite beach or park, or something imagined, like a cozy cabin.

3. Engage all your senses: notice the light, sounds, textures, and smells. Maybe it's the crash of waves, the scent of pine, or the softness of a blanket.

4. As you breathe slowly, picture any anxious money thoughts melting away, replaced by calm.

5. Stay here for 2–3 minutes, then return gently to the present, carrying the calm with you.

Many people find this especially helpful before opening a banking app, checking credit card statements, or starting a money conversation. Even a brief "visit" can interrupt the fight–flight–freeze response and make the task feel more manageable.

Future Self Visualization

This practice helps you connect with who you want to become financially—your wiser, calmer future self.

1. Imagine yourself 5 or 10 years from now, living in alignment with your values.

2. Picture the details: Where are you? What does daily life look like? How do you earn, save, and spend?

3. Notice how this future version of you feels when handling money—maybe steady, proud, or at peace.

4. Ask: What advice would this future self give me about today's worries?

5. Bring back one quality—such as resourcefulness, self-kindness, or patience—and let it guide your next step.

One reader described her "aha moment" during this exercise: *"I realized my future self wouldn't scold me for past mistakes—she'd just encourage me to try again."* This simple shift can dissolve shame and unlock motivation.

Healing Imagery

Sometimes financial stress is tied to old wounds—memories of job loss, debt, or scarcity. Healing imagery allows you to reframe these memories with compassion.

1. Call to mind a painful money memory.

2. Imagine the feeling as something tangible—perhaps a heavy stone or dark cloud.

3. Visualize gently releasing it: letting it float away, dissolve in sunlight, or wash downstream.

4. Replace it with a new image of abundance or strength: golden light, deep roots, or flowing water.

Repeating this practice softens the grip of shame and creates space for resilience.

Anchoring the Experience

To make visualization stick, pair it with a sensory anchor—a candle, a favorite song, or even holding a warm mug of tea. Each time you practice, engage the same anchor. Over time, your body will learn to associate that sound, scent, or object with calm and confidence, helping you carry the benefits into daily life.

Visualization is not about escaping reality. It's about training your nervous system to respond differently, building a foundation of calm so you can face financial challenges with clarity and steadiness.

Money Mindfulness Practice

Journaling and visualization help uncover your patterns and soften your emotional responses. Now, mindfulness adds another layer: learning to pause in the *moment* before, during, or after a financial decision. Instead of reacting on autopilot, mindfulness creates a space where your choices can reflect your real needs and values.

Mindfulness doesn't mean being perfect or controlling every penny—it means noticing what's happening right now with curiosity, not judgment. Over time, these tiny pauses can rewire your brain, reduce stress, and make money feel less overwhelming.

The Mindful Spending Pause

This practice breaks the automatic loop between feeling and purchase.

1. When you feel the urge to spend—whether online, at the store, or even in a café—pause for 30 seconds.

2. Take a breath and ask: *"What am I feeling right now? Am I meeting a true need, or seeking comfort?"*

3. Notice the answer without judgment.

Example: You're scrolling late at night after a hard day, ready to hit *Buy Now*. The pause helps you realize you're looking for relief from stress, not for the shoes in your cart. Even if you still buy them, the awareness is a win—it's the beginning of change.

Gratitude for Needs Met

This exercise shifts focus from scarcity to sufficiency.

Each time you spend on a genuine need—groceries, rent, utilities—pause and think: *"I am grateful I can meet this need."*

Try it unpacking groceries, paying your phone bill, or buying a bus ticket. Instead of money disappearing, you start to see it as a tool that supports your life. Over time, this small ritual can reduce the urge for "filler" purchases and build a sense of enough.

Reflection prompt: *"How does focusing on what I already have change how I feel about money today?"*

Spotting Triggers in Real Time

Instead of only reviewing patterns later, this practice helps you catch emotional triggers in the moment.

1. When a strong urge to spend, avoid, or check out arises, pause.
2. Ask: *"What just triggered me? What story am I telling myself?"*
3. Write a quick note, even one line, to capture it.

Example: You suddenly want a new phone right after hearing a coworker got promoted. Looking closer, you realize the urge isn't about the phone—it's about feeling behind. That insight is powerful: the trigger wasn't technology, it was comparison.

Building Mindful Routines

Mindfulness becomes habit when it's woven into daily life. Try:

- **Morning Intention:** Before opening your phone, set a money focus for the day. Example: *"I'll check my balance with curiosity, not fear."*

- **Evening Reflection:** Jot one quick note about how money showed up today and what you learned.

- **Weekly Ritual:** Spend 10 minutes reviewing expenses with a nonjudgmental lens, noticing both numbers and feelings.

These routines slowly reshape your brain. Neuroscience shows that repeated awareness builds new neural pathways, making mindful habits easier over time.

One reader described her "aha moment": *"After three weeks of mindful pauses, I realized I was no longer avoiding my bank app—I actually opened it with curiosity."*

Mindfulness doesn't erase setbacks. But every pause, every breath, every note of gratitude adds strength to your foundation. Over time, the present moment becomes a place of calm power rather than panic or avoidance.

Consciously Rewriting Your Money Narrative

By now, you've begun noticing your spending triggers and practicing mindful pauses. The next step is to explore something even deeper: the *stories* you tell yourself about money. These inner narratives often run quietly in the background, shaping how you feel, act, and decide—sometimes without you even realizing it.

Everyone has a money story. Maybe it was formed from family sayings like *"We just can't afford nice things"* or cultural messages like *"Rich people are greedy."* Or perhaps it grew from personal experiences of debt, scarcity, or success. Left unexamined, these stories can become limiting beliefs: *"I'm bad with money," "I'll never get ahead,"* or *"I don't deserve financial security."* These phrases may feel like facts, but they're really just old scripts—and they can be rewritten.

Step 1: Name Your Story

Set aside 10 quiet minutes with a pen and paper. Write down three money stories you've caught yourself repeating. Prompts to try:

- *"What do I believe about myself and money?"*
- *"What phrases from my childhood about money still echo in my head?"*
- *"What do I tell myself when I make a financial mistake?"*

Example: *"Every time I overspend, I think, 'I'll never learn.'"* Another: *"I hear my parents' voice saying, 'Money doesn't grow on trees.'"*

Seeing these beliefs on paper helps you separate them from who you are. They're learned messages, not personal truths.

Step 2: Reframe with Compassion

For each limiting belief, write a new, supportive statement that feels believable. Effective affirmations are short, present-tense, and rooted in kindness.

Examples:

- Old story: *"I'll never have enough."*
  → New truth: *"I am learning to create enough for my needs and*

dreams."

- Old story: *"I always make bad money decisions."*
  → New truth: *"I am practicing more thoughtful choices each day."*

These affirmations don't have to be grand or perfect. They just need to plant a seed of possibility.

Step 3: Make It a Daily Practice

Change takes repetition. Neuroscience shows that regularly repeating affirmations helps create new pathways in the brain, making supportive beliefs more automatic over time. Try weaving them into your day:

- Repeat one aloud while brewing your morning coffee.
- Post sticky notes with affirmations on your mirror or laptop.
- Set a phone reminder that pops up midday with your chosen phrase.

Even if it feels awkward or "silly" at first, stick with it for at least 21 days. The discomfort often fades, replaced by small sparks of confidence.

Step 4: The Story Timeline Exercise

To anchor your new beliefs, imagine your life six months from now if you practiced these affirmations daily. Write down a few vivid scenes:

- Paying bills calmly instead of with dread.
- Celebrating a thoughtful purchase without guilt.
- Asking for a raise with steady confidence.

These mental snapshots connect your inner work to real-world benefits, fueling motivation to keep going.

A Note on Resistance

It's normal if this process stirs up discomfort. Many of these stories are tied to childhood, culture, or past hardships. If doubt arises—*"I don't believe this new story yet"*—that's okay. Growth takes time. Even noticing the resistance is progress.

One reader realized that her lifelong fear of spending came from her parents' constant warnings that "there will never be enough." By naming that belief and slowly reframing it, she began to budget with curiosity instead of dread. Over time, she saved enough for a long-delayed vacation—something her old story told her was impossible.

Rewriting your money narrative is not about forcing blind optimism. It's about choosing words that nurture healing, courage, and possibility. With each reframed belief, you create space for healthier financial choices—and prepare yourself for the practical tools of goal-setting and budgeting ahead.

Wrapping Up

Learning to notice your money patterns is not about perfection—it's about awareness. In this chapter, you've practiced shining a light on the hidden forces behind your financial decisions: journaling to uncover emotions, visualization to soothe stress, mindfulness to slow down impulses, and rewriting the old money stories that no longer serve you. Each exercise is a gentle step toward clarity and self-compassion.

The real power of these tools lies in repetition. Every pause before a purchase, every note in your journal, every kind word you choose instead of a critical one is like laying down a new pathway in your brain. Over time, those pathways become familiar routes toward calm, confidence, and better choices.

And remember, you don't have to master every practice at once. In fact, as you move through the **30-Day Money Reset**, you'll return to these tools again and again—sometimes as daily anchors, sometimes as quick resets when stress rises. Think of this chapter as your personal therapy kit: a collection of exercises you can reach for whenever old patterns start creeping back in.

The next step is to take this inner work and begin pairing it with the outer work of financial planning. With a clearer understanding of your emotions and stories, you'll be ready to design a budget and goal-setting system that feels less like punishment and more like freedom. That's where we'll head next.

Your 30-Day Money Reset

Day 11

Identify a Trigger. Notice one situation that sparks stress, guilt, or avoidance around money (like opening bills or talking with a partner). Write it down without judgment.

Day 12

Name the Feeling. When that trigger happens, pause and write down the primary feeling it brings up — anxiety, shame, frustration, or something else.

Day 13

Choose a Calming Response. Decide on one small action you'll take the next time that trigger shows up — a deep breath, a five-minute walk, or journaling before making a decision.

Chapter Seven

Budgeting That Works—For You

Have you ever noticed how some budgeting methods feel natural for one person, but completely impossible for another? Maybe you've tried rigid systems before and felt like you were forcing yourself into someone else's routine. Or perhaps you started strong with a spreadsheet, only to give up a week later when it felt overwhelming. If that sounds familiar, you're not alone.

That's why, in this stage of your **30-Day Money Reset**, we're not handing you "one perfect budget." Instead, we'll explore three different approaches—the traditional envelope system, zero-based budgeting, and values-based budgeting—so you can experiment and notice what actually works for *you*.

Think of this as a 30-day trial period for your budget. You don't need to lock yourself into one method forever. Over the next few weeks, you'll test-drive these approaches, pay attention to how they feel, and adapt them to your unique rhythms.

- Jamie, for instance, loved the tactile comfort of using cash envelopes—it gave her a sense of grounding when swiping cards left her anxious.

- Priya found freedom in zero-based budgeting, where every single dollar had a job and nothing was left unaccounted for.

- Morgan discovered empowerment through values-based budgeting, aligning her money with what mattered most—her creativity, health, and relationships.

These stories aren't just about numbers. They reflect different emotional needs and motivations. As you read, you'll be invited to notice which style feels nurturing rather than restrictive. Do you crave clear boundaries? Do you feel relief when everything is structured, or freedom when your money reflects your values?

By the end of this chapter, you'll have a compassionate map of budgeting styles—and a practical plan to start experimenting with your own during the Reset. This isn't about fitting into someone else's system. It's about discovering a method that meets you where you are today and evolves as you do.

Flexible Budgeting Methods Compared

Choosing a budgeting style can feel overwhelming, especially if past attempts left you frustrated or burned out. But here's the good news: for the purpose of this **30-Day Reset**, you don't need to find the "perfect" system right away. Instead, you'll be experimenting with approaches to see which one fits your life, your habits, and your emotions best. Think of this as a trial run—not a lifelong commitment.

The Envelope System: Tangible Boundaries

The traditional envelope system is one of the oldest and most popular methods because it creates visible, physical boundaries around spending. You assign cash—or its digital equivalent—to categories like groceries, dining out, or entertainment. When the envelope is empty, that's it: no overspending in that category.

This method is grounding for visual and tactile learners who feel more in control when they can literally "see" their money. Jamie, a busy professional, used envelopes for groceries and outings and loved the sense of calm it gave her at the farmers' market. But like many of us, she found carrying cash tricky for online shopping or subscriptions.

That's where modern tools like Goodbudget or Mvelopes apps come in. These digital versions let you create virtual envelopes, track spending in real time, and even share the budget with a partner. For the Reset, you could test this system by choosing just one or two categories to track with envelopes (physical or digital) for a week. Notice how it feels—does the structure feel comforting, or restrictive?

Zero-Based Budgeting: Every Dollar Has a Job

Zero-based budgeting (ZBB) takes a different approach. Here, every dollar of income is assigned a specific purpose—savings, bills, debt payments, groceries—until nothing is left "unaccounted for." There's no room for mystery; every dollar is doing its job.

Priya, for example, sits down at the start of each month, lists her take-home pay, and then distributes every dollar across her categories. This method gave her clarity and reduced her anxiety, because she knew exactly where her money was going.

Zero-based budgeting is powerful for people who crave order, accountability, and a clear sense of control. But it can feel heavy if your life is unpredictable or if you don't enjoy constant updates. For the Reset, you can try a light version: for one week, write down your total income and subtract each expense line by line until you reach zero. Even this short experiment can show you if ZBB feels empowering or exhausting.

Values-Based Budgeting: Aligning Money With Meaning

Values-based budgeting shifts the focus from restriction to intention. Instead of just asking, "How much can I spend?" you ask, "Does this spending reflect what matters most to me?"

Morgan struggled with guilt over spending on art classes. But once she re-framed her budget around her values, she gave herself full permission to invest in creativity—and her motivation skyrocketed.

This approach is especially powerful if you've felt budgeting is suffocating or joyless. During the Reset, you might start by listing your top three values—like health, relationships, or growth—and linking each to one spending category. Then track how much of your money supports those values for a week.

Bringing It Together

There's no single "best" method—only the one that feels workable and sustainable for you. That's why the Reset is structured around experimentation. For the next 30 days, you'll try elements of these three systems and reflect on what feels grounding, motivating, or overwhelming.

Here's a quick guide:

- **Envelope Method** suits those who like tangible boundaries and visual cues.

- **Zero-Based Budgeting** supports detail-oriented planners who want control.

- **Values-Based Budgeting** resonates with people driven by meaning, joy, or creativity.

As you test-drive these styles, keep a gentle eye on your emotions. Do you feel relief? Frustration? Motivation? Those signals are as important as the numbers themselves.

Making Your Budget Fail-Proof

Budgets often collapse not because the math was wrong, but because life happened. A surprise bill, a busy week, or an emotional low point can nudge you off course, and suddenly the whole plan feels "broken." In the **30-Day Reset**, we don't treat those moments as failure—they're simply feedback. A fail-proof budget isn't about being flawless; it's about having enough flexibility, rituals, and self-compassion built in that you can bend without breaking.

Build Flexible Buffer Zones

Think of a buffer as breathing space for both your money and your emotions. By setting aside even 5–10% of your income as a "just-in-case" cushion, you protect yourself from the all-or-nothing thinking that often derails progress.

For someone with freelance income, a buffer might catch the dips between projects. For a parent, it could absorb school fees or an unexpected utility spike. The point is not the exact amount—it's the sense of safety it provides.

Reset Practice: This month, create a small buffer category in your budget, even if it's just $20. Notice how it feels knowing that cushion exists. Relief? Security? Permission to exhale? Write that down—you're building emotional resilience as much as financial.

Schedule Budget "Check-Ins"

Consistency beats intensity. Setting aside a short, regular time to review your budget turns money management into a ritual of care rather than a dreaded chore.

During the Reset, experiment with a weekly check-in. Choose a time that feels calm—maybe Sunday evening with a cup of tea, or Friday morning before the weekend. Keep it simple: open your budget, look at what went well, what felt tricky, and what needs adjusting.

Reflection Prompt: How do you feel before your first check-in—anxious, curious, hopeful? Over time, notice if that feeling shifts toward pride or calm. That's a sign your new rhythm is working.

Use Visual Tracking

Budgets are easier to stick with when you can literally see your progress. Whether it's a hand-drawn thermometer filling up as your savings grow, a pie chart showing where your money flows, or an app's colorful dashboard, visuals give you motivation without judgment.

During the Reset, try creating one visual tracker for a single goal—like debt reduction or building your buffer fund. Each time you make progress, color in a square or move a bar upward.

Aha Moment: Watching your chart fill in slowly transforms abstract numbers into something tangible, and even small wins start to feel real.

Celebrate Small Wins

Too often, we only reward ourselves for big milestones—like paying off a loan or hitting a savings goal. But in reality, lasting change comes from celebrating the small, steady steps along the way.

For the Reset, choose a small, joyful ritual for each weekly win. It might be making your favorite coffee, texting a friend about your progress, or taking a mindful walk. The point isn't the size of the reward—it's the signal you send yourself: *I'm proud of showing up.*

Reflection Prompt: What emotions surface when you mark a win—pride, excitement, maybe even unfamiliar joy? Notice those feelings; they're proof that managing money can feel good, not just stressful.

Bringing It Together

By layering in buffers, check-ins, visuals, and celebrations, you give your budget the flexibility and emotional support it needs to last beyond the 30 days. Each element makes your system softer, more humane, and more sustainable. You're not aiming for perfection—you're building resilience.

Budgeting With Others—Couples & Families

Money isn't just personal—it's relational. If you share finances with a partner or family, your budget becomes more than numbers; it's a reflection of shared priorities, hidden fears, and sometimes unspoken expectations. That's why the **30-Day Reset** invites you to treat collaborative budgeting as both a financial practice and a relationship practice. It's not about agreeing on every dollar—it's about building trust, empathy, and teamwork.

Start with Honest Conversations

Opening up about money can feel vulnerable, especially if past experiences carry shame or conflict. But naming feelings aloud is what turns budgeting into a safe, shared practice.

Reset Step: Schedule one "money talk" this month. Keep it short—20–30 minutes—and set ground rules like: *no blame, no judgment, just listening.* Use prompts such as:

- "What's one thing I'm proud of in how I handle money?"
- "What's one financial worry on my mind?"

You'll be surprised how much relief comes simply from being heard.

Choose a Structure That Fits *You*

Couples and families thrive with different setups. Some pool everything into joint accounts. Others keep separate accounts but share expenses. Many use hybrids—like one joint account for bills and savings, and personal accounts for flexibility.

There's no single "right" way—just the way that reflects your personalities, trust levels, and goals.

Reflection Prompt: Which setup would make you feel more secure? Which would make you feel more free? What emotions surface when you imagine combining finances—or keeping them separate?

Respect Different Priorities

Money talks often reveal differences: one person values travel, another wants to pay down debt, a third (in family settings) is focused on building college savings. These aren't conflicts—they're opportunities for empathy.

Reset Step: Each partner or family member writes down their top three priorities. Then compare. Where do they overlap? Where do they diverge? Agree to fund at least one shared goal, while respecting one personal goal each.

This turns budgeting into collaboration, not competition.

Make It Routine, Not a Crisis

Instead of only talking about money when there's a problem, create a rhythm of regular check-ins. During the Reset, aim for **one joint budget review**—even if it's just once this month. Keep it short, and focus on wins: "We stayed under our grocery budget" or "We added $50 to savings."

Make it lighter with a ritual—play music, share a treat, or close with gratitude. These touches help money conversations feel supportive instead of stressful.

A Note on Families with Kids

If you're budgeting as a family, involving children can build early financial confidence. Give them small allowances or let them track a family savings jar. Celebrate together when you reach a shared goal (like saving for a day trip). Modeling open, non-judgmental conversations teaches kids that money isn't scary—it's something you can handle with care.

Bringing It Together

Collaborative budgeting isn't about perfect alignment. It's about creating a safe space where every voice matters, differences are respected, and shared progress is celebrated. Within the 30-Day Reset, even one honest talk, one shared decision, or one joint win is enough to start transforming money from a source of tension into a tool for connection.

Wrapping Up

Exploring the envelope method, zero-based budgeting, and values-based budgeting is not about choosing the "perfect" approach—it is about discovering which system feels realistic and sustainable for you. Each method offers a different way to bring clarity and confidence to your finances. Some people thrive on the structure of envelopes or zero-based budgeting, while others feel most supported when their spending directly reflects their values.

The truth is, your preferences will shift over time. What works in a season of tight cash flow may need adjusting when your income changes, or when your priorities evolve. That is why flexibility matters just as much as structure.

Within the 30-Day Reset, your goal is not to lock yourself into one rigid budget forever. Instead, you will experiment with one method this month, track your experience, and reflect on what feels supportive. This is about progress, not perfection. By the end of these 30 days, you will have evidence of what works for you in real life, not just in theory.

Take a moment to notice how you feel about budgeting after reading this chapter. Do you feel more open, more equipped, or perhaps still hesitant? All of those responses are valid. What matters most is that you now have tools and options—and the understanding that your emotions and values belong in the process.

Every budget is more than numbers. It is a living reflection of your needs, your goals, and your self-respect. By choosing a method with compassion and flexibility, you are building not only financial clarity but also a practice of self-care that can carry you forward long after the Reset is complete.

Your 30-Day Money Reset

Day 14

Pick Your Method. Choose one budgeting style to try this week — zero-based, 50/30/20, or envelope-style. Don't worry about picking the "perfect" one; just commit to experimenting.

Day 15

Track One Day of Spending. Write down every dollar you spend today, no matter how small. Awareness comes before change.

Day 16

Set Your First Limit. Choose one spending category (like dining out or subscriptions) and decide on a simple weekly or monthly limit. Keep it realistic — the goal is control, not perfection.

Chapter Eight

Debt and Credit: Facing the Past, Shaping the Future

Did you know that nearly 80 percent of Americans carry some form of debt? Credit cards, student loans, personal borrowing, car payments, medical bills—the list goes on. For most people, debt is not rare, it's routine. Yet while debt is common, the emotions that come with it—shame, stress, and silence—can make it feel isolating and overwhelming. Many live with a quiet weight that influences daily choices, moods, and even self-worth.

This chapter of the **30-Day Money Reset** is designed to change that experience. Over the next several days, you'll face debt and credit not as enemies, but as information. By separating facts from shame, you'll learn how to take practical steps toward repayment while also easing the emotional stress that debt often carries. Think of it as creating breathing room: you don't have to solve everything at once—you only need to build clarity and compassion, one step at a time.

Together, we'll explore:

- What different types of debt mean for your financial and emotional life.

- How credit scores really work (and how to improve them without stress).
- Two proven payoff strategies—the snowball and the avalanche—and how to choose which to test this month.
- Tools for healing the anxiety, shame, and self-criticism that often come with owing money.

Within the Reset, you'll devote just one week to this chapter's focus. You'll list your debts with honesty, check your credit report without fear, and experiment with a small action—like choosing a payoff method or practicing a self-compassion exercise—so that progress feels both real and sustainable.

Debt does not define you. It is not a moral failing. It is simply one part of your financial story. By facing it openly and without judgment, you begin to shape a future where money feels manageable, hopeful, and even empowering.

Understanding Debt Without Shame

Everyone's relationship with debt is different, but almost all of us carry some form of emotional baggage with it. For many, credit cards, student loans, or personal loans are not just financial tools—they're reminders of past decisions, unexpected emergencies, or dreams pursued. What they often come with is not just interest, but shame. That shame makes debt harder to face honestly, which is why it lingers in the background of so many lives.

The **30-Day Money Reset** is designed to meet you right there. During this week of the Reset, one of your first small steps will be to look at your debt not as a verdict on your character, but as simple information. This exercise isn't about blame or even quick repayment—it's about clarity. By writing down your debts in one place, you'll transform vague dread into something visible and manageable.

Debt takes different forms, each with its own rules and emotional weight. Credit card debt, for example, is revolving—you can borrow, repay, and borrow again. It can feel like a lifeline in emergencies, but with high interest rates, balances often grow faster than expected. That combination of flexibility and pressure explains why credit cards trigger so much anxiety. Student loans are different: they are typically fixed-term and purpose-driven, covering tuition and living costs. For many, they represent opportunity—access to careers and education that wouldn't otherwise be possible—but they also carry expectations about future earning power. Personal loans fall somewhere in between, often used to consolidate debt, renovate a home, or support a major life change. Their fixed payments can bring clarity, but they also require consistent tracking.

While each type of debt works differently, they share a common emotional thread: self-criticism. It is easy to interpret owing money as proof of irresponsibility, laziness, or failure. But debt itself is neutral—it is simply a tool. Used responsibly, it can bridge gaps, support transitions, or create opportunities. Consider Jenna, who borrowed through a low-interest student loan to change careers in her thirties. Instead of framing it as a setback, she saw it as an investment in her future. That perspective turned a potentially shame-laden choice into a story of resilience and growth.

One day of this week's Reset will be devoted to a reflection exercise: reframing your debt. Instead of asking, "How did I get here?" you'll ask, "What has this debt made possible for me?" You might find pride in being able to pay for safe housing, gratitude for education, or relief from consolidating old bills. Recognizing these truths doesn't mean you want debt forever—it means you stop seeing it as a personal flaw and start approaching it with clarity and self-respect.

Letting go of the fantasy of being completely debt-free can also bring relief. For most people, certain kinds of debt—like mortgages—are part of a balanced financial plan. The Reset helps you shift focus away from perfectionism and toward sustainability. The goal is not "zero debt at any cost" but rather "manageable, conscious debt that supports my real life." When you hold this perspective, repayment becomes less about shame and more about strategy.

As you'll see later in this chapter, pairing this mindset with a personalized budget (Chapter 6) makes repayment far more achievable. With a foundation of self-awareness and compassion, managing debt stops being an exercise in self-blame and becomes a step toward empowerment and agency.

Credit Scores Demystified

If debt carries a heavy load of shame, credit scores often add confusion on top of it. Many people know their score "matters," yet few fully understand how it works. The result? Anxiety, avoidance, or the belief that one number defines your worth. It doesn't. A credit score is not a personal report card—it's simply a measure that lenders use to predict risk. When you learn how it works, you can start to use it as a tool instead of letting it intimidate you.

As part of this **30-Day Money Reset**, one of your small steps this week will be to check your credit report. Not all three bureaus, not every detail at once—just one report from one bureau. The goal isn't to obsess over your score or try to "fix" everything overnight. It's to take one mindful action that turns avoidance into awareness.

Credit scores are built from five key components:

- **Payment history**: The biggest factor. Paying bills on

time—even the minimum—builds trust. Missing payments damages this area, but positive patterns build back over time.

- **Amounts owed**: How much of your available credit you're using. Keeping balances under 30% of your limit is seen as healthy.
- **Length of history**: How long you've had credit accounts. Older accounts help—even if you don't use them often.
- **Types of credit**: A mix (like cards, loans, or mortgages) shows you can manage different responsibilities.
- **New credit**: Too many recent applications can temporarily lower your score.

Here's the Reset perspective: you don't need to master all five areas at once. This month, focus on just one small, practical shift—like setting up an automatic reminder to pay bills on time or making an extra payment on one balance. These actions, repeated consistently, carry more weight than trying to overhaul your entire financial history in a single swoop.

Consider Maya, who avoided her credit report for years because she assumed it would confirm her worst fears. When she finally pulled one, she discovered her oldest credit card—long ignored—was quietly helping her by anchoring her credit history. That small surprise reframed her thinking: she wasn't failing; she had strengths she hadn't even noticed.

During the Reset, you'll also take a few minutes to reflect on how your credit makes you feel. Relief? Shame? Pride? Anxiety? Naming these emotions is just as important as knowing the numbers themselves. When you bring both the facts and the feelings into the open, you can approach your credit with calm instead of fear.

By weaving this step into the Reset—checking one report, noticing one feeling, making one adjustment—you'll discover that credit management doesn't have to be mysterious or punishing. It becomes a normal part of your financial self-care, no more intimidating than a wellness checkup.

Payoff Plans That Stick

Now that you've begun reframing debt as neutral information and taken the first step of checking your credit, it's time to look at practical strategies for paying it down. For many, the hardest part isn't knowing *what* to do—it's staying motivated long enough to see results. That's where the **30-Day Money Reset** provides structure: instead of trying to solve everything at once, you'll spend this week experimenting with repayment methods and choosing the one that feels most sustainable for you.

Two of the most effective—and most widely used—approaches are the **snowball method** and the **avalanche method**. Both work. The key is deciding which one fits *your* psychology.

- **The Snowball Method**: Line up your debts from smallest balance to largest. Pay minimums on all of them, but put any extra cash toward the smallest debt first. Once that's cleared, roll its payment into the next smallest, and so on. The snowball's power comes from momentum. Knocking out one debt quickly creates visible wins and boosts motivation. Many people find this emotional fuel makes it easier to keep going.

- **The Avalanche Method**: Instead of focusing on size, focus on cost. Order debts from highest interest rate to lowest. Pay minimums across the board, but funnel any extra money to the debt with the highest interest first. This method saves you the most money in the long run, but it can take longer to feel the emotional payoff if your highest-interest balance is also your largest.

In the Reset, you won't just read about these—you'll actually test them. One day this week is devoted to running your numbers through both approaches. You'll see how long each strategy might take, how much interest you could save, and which one gives you more peace of mind. For some, the snowball's quick wins are essential; for others, the avalanche's efficiency feels smarter and steadier.

Take Alex, who started with a $300 store card, a $2,000 Visa, and a $6,000 student loan. Using the snowball, she paid off the store card in a single month. That small victory gave her energy to tackle the bigger debts. Priya, on the other hand, owed similar amounts but with a 24% interest credit line. She chose the avalanche, targeting that high-cost debt first. Both approaches worked because each person picked the plan that matched their mindset.

The Reset also encourages you to set up **accountability tools**. This could be a printable tracker where you color in a square for every $50 paid, or an app like Undebt.it that shows progress visually. These tools turn repayment into something you can see and celebrate, even when the finish line still feels far away. One of your tasks during this week is to choose one tool and use it.

To keep your momentum alive, you'll also identify a **celebration ritual**. Maybe it's a favorite coffee after paying off a balance, a short walk, or sharing the win with a friend. Building in these small rewards makes repayment less about deprivation and more about growth.

The truth is, either method works. What matters is sticking with it. By the end of this week in the Reset, you'll not only have chosen your payoff plan—you'll have practiced using it, tracked your progress, and given yourself permission to celebrate along the way. That shift from dread to engagement is where lasting change begins.

Healing Debt-Related Stress: Strategies for Emotional Recovery

Debt doesn't just live on paper. It shows up in your body, your emotions, and your daily choices. Anxiety before opening a bill, shame when swiping a card, or even numbness at the sight of your statements—these are all signs that money stress is running deeper than the numbers. The good news is that stress can be soothed, and healing is possible when you pair practical steps with emotional care. That's why this part of the **30-Day Money Reset** focuses not only on what you *owe*, but on how you *feel*.

One Reset exercise this week asks you to **list your debts on paper, without judgment**. Sit somewhere calm, take a breath, and write each balance down—"$2,200 credit card," "$17,000 student loan"—without adding words like "awful" or "hopeless." Then pause and notice what emotions come up: tightness in the chest, worry in the stomach, maybe even relief at finally seeing things clearly. Simply naming these feelings—"I notice I'm anxious" or "I feel embarrassed"—is powerful. You're no longer avoiding; you're observing.

Next, the Reset guides you to **break the mountain into hills**. Instead of staring at the total, you'll identify one smaller balance or one specific step to focus on. For example, "Today, I'll make a plan for the card with the lowest balance." This shift reframes debt from an overwhelming weight into a series of manageable steps, reducing the panic that often leads to avoidance.

To keep emotions in view alongside the numbers, you'll start a **Debt Recovery Journal**. Each time you make a payment, negotiate a lower interest rate, or stick to your plan, you'll jot down what happened and how it felt. Some entries will celebrate progress ("I paid $100 today and felt proud"), while others will acknowledge challenges ("I avoided looking at my statements this week, but I came back to it"). The Reset reminds you: progress is built on self-compassion, not perfection. Forgiving yourself when you stumble makes it easier to get back up tomorrow.

Support is also part of this Reset week. Debt stress thrives in silence, so one exercise asks you to identify someone safe you could share your situation with—a counselor, a friend, or a supportive online group. You don't have to hand over all your numbers; you can start small, with a script like, "I'm trying to pay off some debt and it feels overwhelming—could I talk it through with you?" That first step often replaces isolation with relief.

If you share finances with a partner or family, the Reset gives you gentle prompts to open conversations: "I feel anxious about our credit card balance and would like to make a plan together," or "Can we set aside one time a week to look at our budget so I don't feel alone in this?" These "I feel" statements keep the focus on emotions instead of blame, building teamwork and connection.

Finally, you'll be invited to reflect with this Reset prompt: **"What does self-compassion look like for me right now?"** Maybe it's forgiving a late payment instead of spiraling into guilt. Maybe it's acknowledging that carrying debt doesn't make you a failure—it makes you human. Each kind response you give yourself is another form of repayment, one that lightens your emotional load while you chip away at the financial one.

By the end of this Reset week, you'll have not only a repayment plan but also emotional tools to manage stress along the way. Because facing debt isn't just about numbers—it's about reclaiming peace of mind, one small, kind step at a time.

Final Thoughts

Debt is one of the heaviest weights people carry—not just financially, but emotionally. This chapter has shown that debt is not a sign of failure or weakness. It's common, it's manageable, and it can even be reframed as a tool that supported you through education, opportunity, or stability when you needed it most.

Through the **30-Day Money Reset**, you've taken the first steps toward changing that relationship. You've learned to see debt without shame, to check your credit report calmly, to explore payoff methods like snowball or avalanche, and to practice emotional recovery when stress arises. None of this requires an overnight fix. Instead, it's about taking small, repeatable actions that move you forward while treating yourself with compassion.

Perfection—the dream of being debt-free tomorrow—was never the goal. Progress is. And progress comes from clear awareness, realistic plans, and consistent follow-through. When you celebrate each payment, each act of self-kindness, and each moment of clarity, you are building resilience as well as financial strength.

As you continue with the Reset, remember this: debt does not define you. It is simply one part of your financial story. By facing it openly, without shame, you reclaim power over your money and create space for the future you want. With every mindful choice, you are not just reducing balances—you are building freedom, confidence, and peace of mind.

Your 30-Day Money Reset

Day 17

List Your Debts. Write down each debt you have — balance, minimum payment, and interest rate if you know it. Seeing it clearly is the first step toward change.

Day 18

Choose Your Payoff Strategy. Decide whether the **snowball method** (smallest debt first) or the **avalanche method** (highest interest first) fits your style best. Commit to trying it.

Day 19

Check Your Credit Report. Visit AnnualCreditReport.com (or the equivalent in your country) and review your report for errors or surprises. Note one step you can take to strengthen your credit health.

Chapter Nine

Saving and Investing: Building Your Financial Foundation

Imagine a life where the sudden worry of an unexpected bill no longer grips you with anxiety because you've created a cushion of savings. This safety net not only shields you from financial shocks but also nurtures your personal dreams and goals. Picture your money quietly working for you, growing steadily through thoughtful investments that reflect what matters most to you. This is more than numbers—it's about security, empowerment, and hope for what lies ahead, built through consistent, intentional action.

In the **30-Day Money Reset**, this chapter marks a shift. Earlier, you focused on awareness, budgeting, and tackling debt. Now you begin building stability through savings and long-term growth through investing. Together, these habits form the foundation of your financial reset: protection for today and confidence for tomorrow.

Saving for Security and Opportunity

Feeling nervous about saving is common. Many people believe saving means cutting out joy or living under strict limits. In reality, saving can be reframed as self-care. Financial stress often comes from lacking a cushion when life throws surprises your way. Each deposit—no matter how small—helps reduce anxiety and sends a clear message: *I'm taking care of myself.*

An emergency fund is the cornerstone of this security. It's money set aside for life's unexpected moments—a medical bill, a job loss, or urgent car repairs. Imagine waking up to a flat tire. Without savings, panic sets in and you may turn to debt. With even a modest fund, the same situation becomes manageable. Experts recommend aiming for three to six months of essential expenses: rent, groceries, utilities, insurance, and loan payments. But in the Reset, you start with what feels possible. A first target might be $500 or one month's rent. Even $10 a week builds the saving habit, and over time, that habit matters more than the number itself.

One Reset reader set up a $15 weekly transfer and after a year had accumulated $700. When an unexpected dental bill arrived, they were able to pay it outright—avoiding debt and experiencing, for the first time, the relief of being financially prepared.

Keep your emergency fund in an account that's easy to access in an emergency but not so convenient you're tempted to dip into it casually. High-yield savings accounts often offer better interest than basic savings while keeping money safe. Look for accounts with no monthly fees and easy online access.

Beyond emergencies, savings also create opportunities. Short-term goals might include replacing a phone, planning a trip, or setting aside for holiday expenses. Long-term goals might be a down payment on a home, funding education, or building retirement security. Both matter. If you're living paycheck-to-paycheck, saving toward something small—a pair of shoes, a family celebration—can be as important emotionally as saving for the future. Choose one short-term and one long-term goal to focus on, and record why each matters to you.

Allocating deposits across goals provides balance. For example, you might send $7 per week to your emergency fund and $3 toward a weekend treat. Splitting savings this way builds pride and allows you to see progress across different needs.

Automating transfers removes the need for willpower and makes saving consistent. Most banks allow you to set a recurring transfer from checking to savings on payday. Start with a number that feels realistic, knowing you can adjust it later. Once automation is in place, you'll likely notice the money less, and your balance will grow in the background. One Reset participant set up $20 weekly transfers and was surprised to find over $1,000 in savings a year later—without feeling deprived along the way.

Checking in monthly helps you adjust without rigidity. If income changes, modify the transfer amount rather than abandoning the habit. Flexibility keeps your plan sustainable.

Finally, recognize your progress. Celebrate hitting milestones, whether that's $100, $500, or more. Small rewards—like a special meal or updating a visual tracker—reinforce the habit. These moments aren't indulgence; they're fuel. Progress builds motivation, which is central to making your Reset stick.

No two saving journeys look alike, and missed contributions aren't failures—they're learning opportunities. The key is persistence and self-compassion. With these habits in place, you've built the financial muscle needed for the next step: letting your money work for you through investing.

Investing 101: Making Your Money Work

It's normal to feel uneasy about moving from saving to investing. Savings accounts feel safe; investing involves uncertainty, jargon, and stories of both great wins and painful losses. Many people hesitate for years, believing investing is only for experts or the wealthy. But the truth is, investing is about consistent habits, not complex strategies. If you've already automated savings or built an emergency fund during this Reset, you have the skills you need to take the next step.

At its core, investing means using your money to buy assets—stocks, bonds, mutual funds, or real estate—with the goal of building wealth over time. Unlike savings accounts, which prioritize safety but offer limited growth, investing uses tools like **compound interest** and market growth to help your money multiply.

Here's the difference: imagine setting aside $50 each month. In a savings account, low interest might only add a few dollars a year. Place that same amount into a diversified investment fund, and thanks to compounding—the growth of earnings on both your deposits and on previous gains—your balance has the potential to grow far faster. Investing not only protects your money from inflation but also moves you closer to bigger dreams like home ownership, retirement, or extended travel.

Understanding Risk

The hesitation around investing usually comes down to risk. Savings accounts feel certain, while markets rise and fall. Recognizing that all investments involve some level of uncertainty helps, but not all risks are equal:

- **Cash savings** are the safest, with little chance of loss, but they also provide the lowest return.

- **Certificates of deposit (CDs)** offer slightly higher returns, but your money is locked up for a set period.
- **Bonds** (loans to governments or companies) usually pay moderate interest with lower volatility than stocks.
- **Stocks** (ownership in companies) are riskier because prices can swing, but over the long term, they've historically offered higher rewards.

The goal isn't to eliminate risk but to match your choices with your comfort level and time horizon. For someone who values predictability, bonds may feel better than volatile tech stocks. For others, accepting some short-term ups and downs is worth the long-term growth.

Choosing the Right Accounts

Where you invest matters as much as what you invest in. Different accounts serve different goals:

- **Retirement accounts** (401(k)s, IRAs, or equivalents) offer tax advantages but limit access until a certain age.
- **Brokerage accounts** provide flexibility and are useful for medium-term goals or general wealth building, though without built-in tax breaks.

Choosing the right account depends on your goals, timeline, and whether you'd benefit from tax incentives.

The Power of Starting Small

A common barrier is the belief that you need thousands of dollars to begin. In reality, **starting small and starting early** beats waiting for the "perfect" moment. Even $20 a week invested in a broad index fund can grow meaningfully over time. One Reset participant began this way at age 29. After three years, her steady contributions, plus modest market growth, added up to a balance that exceeded what she thought possible from "small" deposits.

The lesson: consistency matters more than perfection. Waiting until you feel fully prepared often leads to never starting. Taking action—even modest action—signals commitment to your financial future and builds confidence step by step.

Where This Fits in the Reset

By Day 20 of the Reset, most participants have built an emergency fund and begun automating savings. Investing is the next layer—transforming stability into growth. Just as you automated savings, you'll automate small investment contributions. Just as you tracked your spending, you'll begin tracking your investments. Each step builds on the last, creating a system you can live with.

The 30-Day Money Reset doesn't expect you to become a professional investor. The goal is simpler: give you the knowledge, confidence, and habits to get started in a way that feels safe and sustainable. From here, we'll explore how to align investments with your values and overcome the barriers that hold many people back.

Aligning Investments With Your Values

Once you've taken your first steps into investing, it's natural to pause and ask: *What does my money support?* Beyond numbers on a statement, every dollar invested has influence. It funds the companies, industries, and projects that shape the world. Aligning your investments with your values means your financial growth supports not just your future but also the kind of future you want to see around you.

This is where the Reset encourages you to think beyond mechanics. You've already learned to save consistently and automate habits. Now you're invited to bring self-awareness into investing so your portfolio reflects your priorities as much as your financial goals.

The Basics of ESG Investing

A growing area of values-driven investing is ESG: Environmental, Social, and Governance.

- **Environmental (E):** companies working to reduce pollution, embrace renewable energy, or protect natural resources.

- **Social (S):** businesses that treat employees fairly, promote diversity, or support communities.

- **Governance (G):** firms committed to transparency, strong leadership, and ethical decision-making.

Investing with ESG criteria allows you to channel your money toward organizations that act responsibly while still pursuing long-term growth. Ratings agencies like MSCI and Morningstar offer sustainability scores, making it easier to compare funds and companies.

Making It Personal

The starting point is self-reflection. Take a few minutes to jot down the issues that matter most to you—climate action, gender equality, animal welfare, economic fairness, or another cause close to your heart. With those priorities in mind, you can begin filtering investment options. Many online brokerages now provide ESG screeners so you can search for funds and stocks that align with your values.

For example, if clean energy matters to you, you might look for funds focused on renewable technology. If diversity and equity are priorities, you could research funds that invest in companies with inclusive leadership. These decisions turn investing from a purely financial exercise into one that also reflects your principles.

Keeping Alignment Over Time

Values evolve as life changes. That's why part of the Reset approach is not just to choose investments once but to review them periodically. Scheduling a check-in once or twice a year gives you the chance to ask: *Do my investments still reflect what I believe in?* Adjustments may be small—redirecting new contributions or shifting a portion of your portfolio—but over time, they create a portfolio that feels authentic to who you are.

Balancing Purpose and Performance

It's true that prioritizing values can sometimes mean giving up short-term gains. Yet, values-aligned companies may also face fewer long-term risks—such as scandals, fines, or reputational damage—making them resilient investments. Blending high-growth funds with ESG-friendly ones can give you both stability and impact.

The important thing is choice. When your investments align with your values, you experience more than financial growth—you gain a sense of pride and calm knowing your money is working in ways that matter to you.

Support and Simplicity

You don't need to research every company on your own. Many digital platforms now offer ESG-focused portfolios tailored to your risk level, making it easier to invest with confidence. Independent ratings and online communities also provide guidance, encouragement, and accountability.

What matters most in the Reset isn't building a perfect portfolio overnight, but taking intentional steps to ensure your financial growth matches your personal compass. Each decision, however small, reinforces the link between your money, your values, and your future.

Overcoming Common Barriers to Investing

By the time you reach this stage of the Reset, you've already built savings habits and taken first steps toward investing. But it's normal if hesitation lingers. Many people never invest because of deeply rooted fears or myths—often absorbed from past experiences or cultural messages. The goal here isn't to dismiss those feelings, but to face them directly so they lose their power.

The Fear of Loss

One of the strongest barriers is the fear of losing money. Research shows losses feel roughly twice as painful as gains feel rewarding. If you've seen family or friends lose money in the markets, or if you've personally faced financial instability, it's natural for this fear to feel real and immediate.

The Reset approach reframes loss as part of the process—not something to eliminate, but something to manage. The most effective tool here is diversification: spreading your investments across different types of assets (stocks, bonds, funds, or even real estate). With diversification, a setback in one area doesn't wipe out your progress in another. Instead of gambling everything on a single outcome, you're balancing risks so no single event derails your future.

A practical Reset exercise: Write down three things you fear most about investing. Then, next to each, note whether that fear is based on a real experience, something you've heard from others, or just uncertainty about the unknown. This small act of naming your fears often makes them easier to manage.

"Too Late" and "Not Enough"

Two of the most common myths about investing are: *It's too late for me to start,* and *I don't have enough money to make it worthwhile.* Both are untrue.

Time in the market matters far more than timing the market. Even small, regular contributions build up meaningfully through the power of compounding. Starting with $25 a month today is more valuable than waiting until you feel "ready" years from now.

One Reset participant delayed investing until her mid-thirties because she believed small amounts wouldn't matter. When she finally began, she was surprised how quickly even modest deposits grew into something substantial. The lesson: the size of your first step matters less than the fact that you took it.

Building Confidence Gradually

Confidence in investing isn't instant; it grows with practice and learning. You don't need to know everything before you begin. Free resources—from beginner-friendly articles and videos to apps that simulate investing without risk—can help build familiarity step by step. Online communities and peer groups also provide reassurance that you're not navigating this path alone.

The Reset encourages you to choose one learning activity this week: read an introductory article, test a simulator app, or ask a trusted friend how they began. Note what you discover and how it shifts your outlook. Each small piece of knowledge replaces uncertainty with clarity.

Turning Intention Into Action

The final barrier is perfectionism—the idea that you must have the perfect plan before starting. In reality, progress comes from action. The Reset guides you to break the process down:

1. Choose one goal (a home, retirement, or simply growing wealth).

2. Decide on a timeline that fits your life.

3. Select an amount you can set aside each month.

4. Automate contributions so the habit carries itself forward.

5. Review every few months to check progress and make small adjustments.

When investing becomes part of your regular system—just like automated savings or mindful spending—it no longer feels intimidating. Instead, it becomes another expression of self-care and long-term planning.

Bringing It All Together

Saving and investing aren't just technical steps—they're the foundation of long-term stability and growth. By reframing saving as an act of self-care, you've seen how even the smallest contributions can reduce financial stress and create a sense of calm. With those habits in place, investing becomes the natural next step: a way to let your money work alongside you, supporting both your goals and your values.

Through this chapter, the Reset has guided you to:

- Build a safety net through consistent saving, protecting yourself from life's surprises.
- Explore investing in clear, approachable terms, starting small and steady rather than waiting for perfection.
- Consider how your values can shape your portfolio, so your financial growth reflects the life you want to create.
- Recognize and work through common barriers—fear, perfectionism, or self-doubt—by replacing them with practical tools and steady habits.

The key takeaway is that progress doesn't come from a single dramatic leap but from small, repeatable actions. Automating a weekly transfer, setting a reminder to review your accounts, or making your first modest investment are all steps that compound—not just financially, but emotionally—building confidence, resilience, and clarity.

Your 30-Day Money Reset

Day 20

Open (or Check) Your Savings Account. If you don't have one, set up a separate savings account. If you do, review the balance and write down your current total — no judgment, just awareness.

Day 21

Set a Mini Savings Goal. Choose one short-term goal, like $250 for emergencies or $100 toward a weekend trip. Write it down and commit to a weekly contribution, no matter how small.

Day 22

Take Your First Investment Step. Research one beginner-friendly investment account (brokerage, IRA, or retirement plan) and write down how you'd start. If you already have one, log in and note your current holdings.

Chapter Ten

Navigating Financial Transitions — Career, Family, and Life Changes

Keeping track of your progress is one of the simplest ways to stay motivated—but it's also one of the most easily overlooked. Too often, people only measure success by hard numbers: the size of their savings account, how quickly debt is paid down, or how much their net worth has grown. Those numbers matter, but they never tell the whole story. Progress also includes the invisible shifts—the way you feel when you check your bank balance, the confidence you carry into a money conversation, or the calm that replaces the panic you used to feel when a bill arrived.

That's why reflection needs to be both practical **and** emotional. When you track both sides, you not only see growth on paper, but you also feel it in your body and mindset. This dual awareness is what turns financial change from a short-lived effort into a lasting transformation.

Creating a "Money and Mood" Ritual

One way to bring this balance into your life is by establishing a simple review ritual. Think of it less as an audit and more as a check-in with yourself. Once a month—or even every two weeks if that feels better—set aside a quiet moment to review two things side by side: your numbers and your emotions.

Here's a structure you can try:

- **Step 1: Check the numbers.** Note your current balances (savings, checking, debt, investments). Record income and major expenses from the past period.

- **Step 2: Check your emotions.** Pause and ask: *How do I feel looking at these numbers?* Calm? Nervous? Proud? Frustrated? Write down the first words that come to mind without judgment.

- **Step 3: Spot patterns.** Did certain spending decisions bring joy or regret? Did you notice less stress because bills were paid on time? Do you feel more confident talking about money than you did a month ago?

- **Step 4: Capture wins—financial and emotional.** Write down at least one tangible financial win (like an extra payment toward debt or a new savings milestone) and one emotional win (such as saying no without guilt or checking your bank app without dread).

When you make this a routine, your progress becomes visible in two dimensions. You see the numbers moving in the right direction, but you also feel the emotional weight lifting.

The Power of Small Emotional Wins

Not all victories show up on a spreadsheet. Some of the most powerful shifts are internal. Maybe you finally opened a savings account you'd been putting off, or you asked your employer about retirement contributions for the first time. Maybe you realized you didn't panic when an unexpected expense came up because you had a small buffer in place.

These "quiet wins" are often the ones that stick. Over time, they rewire your brain to see money management not as a source of fear but as a form of self-care. Recognizing and celebrating them is as important as tracking the dollars.

Journaling for Deeper Awareness

A dedicated money journal can help you capture both numbers and emotions in one place. Each entry could include:

- Current account balances
- One financial decision you're proud of
- One moment that felt difficult or stressful
- What you learned from both experiences
- A confidence rating (1–5) for how in control you felt this month

Looking back over several months, you'll start to see patterns. Maybe you notice that stress spikes every time your schedule gets overloaded, leading to impulse spending. Or maybe you see that automating savings reduced your anxiety by half. These insights give you clues about where to focus next.

Reset Reflection

Here's where the **30-Day Reset** comes back into play. Each daily challenge throughout this book was designed to build momentum. Tracking your financial and emotional progress is how you make sure that momentum doesn't stop when the 30 days end. Think of this as the bridge between short-term resets and long-term resilience.

Building Lasting Financial and Emotional Resilience

Once you've learned to track both your numbers and your emotions, the next step is building resilience—the ability to recover quickly from setbacks, adapt to change, and continue moving forward. This is where your financial wellness journey shifts from temporary fixes to lasting transformation.

Resilience isn't about never making mistakes or never feeling stressed about money. It's about what happens next. Do you spiral into guilt and avoidance, or do you pause, reflect, and take one small step in a better direction? With the right tools, resilience turns every setback into a lesson and every success into fuel for the future.

Learning From Slips Without Shame

Setbacks are inevitable: a missed bill, an unexpected expense, or an impulse purchase that derails your budget. The old response might have been shame or harsh self-criticism—"I'll never get this right." But shame drains energy and makes progress harder. Resilience reframes the moment: "I slipped, but what can I learn from it?"

For example, if you notice you tend to overspend after a stressful week, the solution might not be stricter rules—it could be adding a stress-relief ritual that doesn't cost money, like a walk, journaling, or calling a friend. Each slip becomes data, not a definition of failure.

A practical reset here is to keep a **Setback Journal**. Each time something doesn't go to plan, write down:

1. What happened
2. What triggered it
3. What I felt
4. One adjustment I can try next time

Over time, you'll see patterns and solutions emerge, helping you adapt without self-blame.

Managing Financial Stress Proactively

Stress is one of the biggest threats to financial health. When anxiety runs high, people avoid bills, delay decisions, or spend impulsively to cope. Building resilience means learning to manage stress before it takes control.

Here are a few practical tools you can use immediately:

- **Grounding breath before tasks:** Before logging into your bank app, pause and take three deep breaths—in for four counts, hold for four, exhale for four. This lowers your body's stress response and makes it easier to face the numbers.
- **Body scan reset:** Take two minutes to mentally scan from head to toe, noticing tension without judgment. This helps you identify where stress lives in your body and release it.
- **Movement pairing:** Connect a financial task with movement. Review your budget, then reward yourself with a short walk or

stretch. This retrains your brain to associate money tasks with relief instead of dread.

- **Conversation boundaries:** If money talks with a partner or family member escalate, agree on a "pause" phrase—something you can say to take a break before emotions run too high.

These small techniques reduce financial stress in real time, giving you more space to make intentional choices instead of reactive ones.

Fostering a Growth Mindset

Resilience also grows when you see money as a skill—not a fixed trait you're born with. This is the essence of a growth mindset: believing that your abilities improve through effort, practice, and learning.

Instead of saying, "I'm just bad with money," try, "I'm still learning how to manage money in ways that work for me." That one word—"yet"—can completely shift your perspective.

Consider the story of Sienna, a freelancer who used to panic whenever her income dipped. Instead of labeling herself as "bad with money," she reframed slow months as opportunities to practice adaptive budgeting. She built a small buffer, learned to track seasonal patterns, and slowly transformed her stress into confidence.

Adopting a growth mindset makes challenges less threatening. They're no longer evidence of failure but stepping stones toward mastery.

The Role of Affirmations and Self-Talk

How you speak to yourself during financial stress can either build or break resilience. Research shows that affirmations—when specific and believable—help replace negative self-talk with encouragement.

Try a few of these to reinforce resilience:

- "I am capable of adapting to financial challenges."
- "Mistakes are lessons, not verdicts."
- "Every step forward matters, even small ones."
- "I can manage money with patience and confidence."
- "My worth is not measured by my balance sheet."

Write down two or three that resonate most with you. Say them daily for 30 days, and note how your attitude shifts. This practice strengthens the mental muscles you'll rely on when setbacks come.

The Reset Connection

Resilience is where the **30-Day Reset** truly proves its power. Each daily challenge you've completed has trained you to take consistent, bite-sized action. That consistency is what builds resilience. Even when you stumble, you now have a framework: pause, reflect, reset, and move forward. Over 30 days, this repetition rewires both your habits and your self-belief, making it easier to bounce back when life gets messy.

Integrating Emotional Growth with Financial Wellness

Financial health is not just about numbers on a spreadsheet. It's about alignment—making sure the way you handle money reflects your values, your needs, and the person you want to become. Emotional growth and financial planning are not two separate paths; when woven together, they create the foundation for lasting stability and peace of mind.

This integration work is the final layer of your journey. It's where the healing you've done—challenging old beliefs, learning to pause before reacting, setting boundaries—shows up in your day-to-day financial decisions. The goal is not perfection, but harmony: money choices that reduce stress, strengthen self-worth, and support the life you want to live.

Journaling as a Bridge Between Feelings and Finances

One of the most effective tools for integration is reflective journaling. Numbers alone can't tell you *why* you spend, save, or avoid certain tasks—but your emotions can. By regularly writing down your financial experiences, you start to see the connection between thought, feeling, and behavior.

Try prompts like these:

- "What emotions came up for me when I reviewed my bank account this week?"
- "When did I feel most in control of my money, and what was I doing at that time?"
- "Which choice felt most aligned with my values?"
- "What old narrative about money surfaced, and how did I respond differently than before?"

The goal isn't to create perfect entries, but to capture honesty. Over time, you'll notice shifts: fewer moments of panic, more moments of calm; less guilt, more self-encouragement. These observations matter just as much as hitting financial milestones.

Visualization and Values Alignment

Visualization helps bridge the gap between your current reality and the financial life you want to build. Close your eyes and picture a milestone you're working toward: maybe it's debt-free living, a fully funded emergency account, or taking your first family vacation paid in cash. Now go deeper—what does that moment *feel* like? Relief? Pride? Joy? Gratitude?

When you tie emotions to goals, you create stronger motivation. The finish line stops being abstract numbers and becomes an experience worth striving for. For example, someone who visualizes their emergency fund not just as "$1,000 saved," but as "peace when the car breaks down" is more likely to stay consistent.

Use this technique with any financial decision. Before you swipe your card or make an investment, pause and ask: *Does this choice align with the future I want and the values I hold?* Over time, this builds a natural filter—guiding your money to support what truly matters.

Breaking Free From Comparison

One of the biggest emotional traps in money management is comparison. Seeing peers, siblings, or strangers online with bigger homes, nicer cars, or larger savings accounts can trigger shame and scarcity. Integration means reframing this habit.

Instead of comparing yourself to others, return to your own story. Your financial wellness plan is rooted in your values, your priorities, your life. What's meaningful to you may not look like someone else's "success"—and that's not only okay, it's essential.

A practical exercise: Write down three financial wins from the past year that mattered to *you* (no matter how small). Then ask: Would these still feel valuable even if no one else knew about them? If the answer is yes, you're living authentically with your money.

Sharing Growth to Strengthen It

Integration is easier when it's not done in isolation. Trusted conversations with supportive people reinforce your progress and create accountability. Share one or two reflections with a mentor, a close friend, or a partner who understands your journey.

This doesn't mean exposing all your financial details—it means choosing what feels safe and valuable. For example: "I've started to track my emotions with my spending, and I realized I buy more when I'm stressed. I'm working on healthier coping strategies." Conversations like this normalize financial reflection and help you feel less alone.

Over time, sharing small wins strengthens identity. You stop seeing yourself as someone who "can't handle money" and start seeing yourself as someone who is actively growing, healing, and leading change in your own life.

The Reset Connection

This stage is where the **30-Day Reset** becomes a lifelong tool. Each challenge you completed taught you to pair emotional awareness with financial action: noticing triggers, setting boundaries, or practicing reflection. Integration is simply the extension of that—continuing to let your emotions guide smarter decisions.

When you journal through the Reset, visualize your goals, or check in on your values at the end of the day, you're practicing integration in real time. Over 30 days, these practices create a model you can repeat any time you need to reset—whether after a setback, during a big life change, or at the start of a new year.

Crafting Your Personalized Financial Wellness Plan: Integrating Habits and Healing

By now, you've built a foundation of emotional awareness, practical skills, and steady routines. The final step is weaving these threads into a personalized wellness plan—a living guide that helps you sustain progress long after the last page of this book. Think of it not as a rigid checklist, but as a compass: a set of practices that keep you grounded, motivated, and adaptable through life's changes.

Why You Need a Personalized Plan

A one-size-fits-all approach doesn't work in finance, because no two people's lives, values, or resources are identical. A single parent managing childcare expenses has different needs than someone starting their first career, just as a retiree's priorities differ from a young professional's. Your financial wellness plan should reflect *your* story. The goal is to design something you can return to again and again—an anchor that balances both your practical money tasks and your emotional well-being.

A strong plan:

- Keeps your priorities front and center.
- Blends emotional care with financial habits.
- Allows flexibility when life changes.

- Provides structure without creating shame or perfectionism.

Building the Core Checklist

Start by dividing your plan into two categories: **financial practices** and **emotional practices**. Each should be simple, specific, and measurable.

Financial Practices may include:

- Review income and expenses twice per month.
- Maintain automatic transfers into savings or investments.
- Check debt balances monthly and track progress.
- Revisit financial goals quarterly and adjust if needed.
- Review insurance, benefits, and retirement accounts annually.

Emotional Practices may include:

- Journal about money-related emotions once per week.
- Practice a 5-minute grounding technique before reviewing finances.
- Identify one financial "win" each month and celebrate it.
- Reflect on whether money choices aligned with your values this week.
- Schedule one check-in conversation with a trusted friend or partner.

Together, these habits keep both sides of the equation balanced: the numbers and the feelings.

The Annual Financial Retreat

One of the most powerful tools in your plan can be a yearly financial retreat. This doesn't mean a luxury getaway—it's simply a dedicated block of time to pause, reflect, and reset.

Here's how:

1. **Set the stage:** Choose a quiet afternoon, turn off notifications, and prepare a comfortable space with snacks, tea, or music.
2. **Review the past year:** Look at your financial records and journal notes. What progress did you make? Which challenges taught you something important?
3. **Update your goals:** Adjust for new life circumstances, whether that's career shifts, family changes, or personal milestones.
4. **Reflect emotionally:** Ask, "How has my relationship with money changed this year?" or "What beliefs do I want to carry forward, and which ones do I want to leave behind?"
5. **Recommit to habits:** Refresh your core checklist, adding or removing practices as needed.

An annual retreat is your reset button—a way to ensure your financial wellness plan evolves with you instead of becoming stale or irrelevant.

Gentle Accountability

Accountability is crucial, but it should never feel like punishment. Instead of rigid rules, build systems of encouragement. Examples include:

- Setting calendar reminders with positive notes ("Review savings today—celebrate every step forward").

- Sharing small wins with a trusted accountability partner.
- Using a progress tracker that includes both numbers and emotions.
- Recording short voice memos about how you feel after paying off debt or reaching a savings goal.

This kind of accountability keeps you motivated without feeding guilt.

Writing Your Empowered Money Story

The last piece of your plan is narrative. Facts and numbers matter, but story shapes how you see yourself. Write down your **Empowered Money Story**—a short statement of where you've come from, what you've learned, and where you're heading.

For example:

- "I grew up fearing money, but I am learning to trust myself with it. I've built savings and set boundaries, and I know setbacks won't stop me from moving forward."
- "My money story used to be defined by scarcity. Now, I'm creating a future rooted in self-worth, resilience, and balance."

Revisit this story often—at your annual retreat, at the end of each 30-Day Reset, or whenever old doubts resurface. Updating it reminds you that financial growth is an ongoing process, not a one-time event.

The Reset Connection

Your **30-Day Reset Challenges** give structure to this plan. Each one—whether focused on boundaries, budgeting, or emotional awareness—has been a building block. By stringing these resets together, you create a repeatable system you can return to any time life feels overwhelming.

Think of your plan as a cycle:

- **Daily practices** keep you grounded.
- **Monthly check-ins** keep you accountable.
- **Annual retreats** give you perspective.
- **Resets** give you a fresh start whenever you need one.

This layered approach ensures you're not just surviving financially, but continually building resilience, peace, and self-trust.

Bringing It All Together

Sustaining success is not about achieving a perfect balance sheet or eliminating all mistakes. It's about creating a rhythm you can live with—habits that feel supportive, boundaries that protect your well-being, and practices that bring clarity rather than shame. Over the course of this chapter, you've learned how to:

- Track both financial and emotional progress with compassion.
- Build resilience by treating setbacks as learning opportunities, not failures.
- Integrate emotional growth with financial routines, making choices that reflect your values.
- Craft a personalized financial wellness plan that evolves as your life changes.

Taken together, these tools give you not just a system, but a way of living that keeps you grounded when challenges arise and motivated when progress feels slow. Each step is meant to be revisited—not once, but again and again—until the habits become second nature.

This is also where the **30-Day Reset Challenges** come full circle. Each reset offered throughout the book was a way to practice, in real time, the principles you've been learning. Small, consistent changes—not grand overhauls—are what rewire your habits and shift the way you relate to money. By continuing to weave these resets into your daily life, you build a structure that is flexible enough to handle change yet strong enough to carry you forward.

As you close this chapter, pause and acknowledge how far you've come. You now have the knowledge, the tools, and the emotional resilience to keep writing your empowered money story. The journcy does not end here—it expands, shaped by your choices and strengthened by the compassion you bring to yourself along the way.

Your 30-Day Money Reset

Day 23: Notice What Strengthened

Reflect on how holding your boundary changed you.
What became clearer? What became easier? What became non-negotiable?
Confidence grows every time you act in alignment with your values.

Day 24: Share One Financial Win

Tell someone supportive about a financial shift you're proud of — no matter how small.
Speaking your progress out loud makes it real.
It reinforces that you are a woman who takes action.

Day 25: Let Your Progress Land

Pause long enough to acknowledge what you've built these past few weeks.

Awareness. Systems. Choices. Confidence.

Let yourself *feel* the momentum you've created — it's the foundation of your next level.

Chapter Eleven

Sustaining Success

The first 30 days gave you structure, clarity, and a powerful reset. By now, you've seen firsthand how small daily actions create momentum, whether it was tracking your spending, tackling debt, or practicing one boundary around money. But the real test comes after the reset ends. What happens in the weeks and months that follow determines whether your progress becomes a short-term experiment or the foundation of lasting financial well-being.

This chapter is about moving beyond *quick wins* and into *sustainable systems*. It's about shifting from "doing the 30-Day Reset" to "living the reset mindset" every day. Success doesn't depend on perfection—it depends on consistency, self-compassion, and steady course corrections when life inevitably throws you off balance.

The truth is, many people experience a burst of progress at the start of a financial plan only to slide back into old habits once the initial excitement fades. Budgets get ignored. Resets are forgotten. Self-doubt creeps in. That's not failure—it's human nature. The difference between those who sustain success and those who slip back is not willpower, but having systems, rituals, and boundaries in place to carry them forward.

In this final chapter, you'll learn:

- How to track both financial and emotional progress in a way that keeps you motivated.

- The most common pitfalls that undo progress—and how to avoid them.
- How to extend the reset beyond 30 days with quarterly reviews, annual retreats, and mini resets.
- The role of identity in financial success—how to shift from "trying" to "being."
- Ways to pass your progress on to others, deepening your own habits while helping your community.

By the end, you'll not only have a toolkit for sustaining your progress—you'll also see how to transform the 30-Day Reset into a way of life.

Tracking Progress with Self-Compassion

Sustaining your financial reset begins with awareness. Numbers matter, but they're only half the story. To truly measure progress, you must track not just your financial outcomes but also your emotional state and mindset. Think of this as keeping two ledgers: one for money, one for well-being.

Most people default to tracking dollars—savings balances, credit card payments, or investment growth. Those metrics are important, but by themselves they can create pressure, shame, or perfectionism. You might hit a savings goal yet still feel anxious every time you check your balance. You might pay off a credit card and immediately slip into guilt when new expenses arise. Without an emotional check-in, the numbers can mislead you into thinking progress is purely financial.

A better approach is a **"money and mood" ritual**: a regular review that blends the practical with the personal. This ritual should be gentle, intentional, and non-judgmental. For example:

1. **Set the environment.** Choose a consistent time—perhaps the first Sunday of each month. Sit somewhere quiet, make a cup of tea, and treat the ritual as self-care, not punishment.

2. **Review the numbers.** Look at income, expenses, savings, and debt changes. Keep a simple log of key figures rather than dozens of categories.

3. **Check in emotionally.** Ask: *How did I feel when I spent money this month? Which decisions brought relief, and which brought tension? Did I avoid looking at bills, or did I feel steady when I opened my accounts?*

4. **Rate confidence.** On a scale of 1–5, note your current sense of confidence about money. Track this monthly; often the emotional score rises long before the numbers do.

5. **Celebrate non-financial wins.** Maybe you said no to a purchase that once triggered guilt. Maybe you checked your balance without dread. These victories deserve recognition.

Journaling Prompts for Reflection

To deepen your awareness, use prompts like:

- "What's one money choice this month I feel proud of?"

- "What spending triggered stress, and why?"

- "Did I treat myself with kindness when I stumbled?"

- "What did I learn about my relationship with money that I didn't see before?"

Keep your notes in a small journal or digital document. Over time, these entries become a mirror of growth—showing not just rising savings but softer shoulders, steadier moods, and a calmer nervous system.

Real-World Example

Consider Jason, who once avoided opening credit card statements. As part of his reset, he created a monthly check-in where he simply logged balances and rated his stress level from 1–5. At first, the numbers barely changed, but his stress rating dropped steadily. Six months later, his balances were lower *and* his confidence had doubled. Tracking emotions alongside numbers gave him the resilience to stick with it long enough to see real change.

The point isn't perfection. It's progress with compassion. By pairing data with self-understanding, you transform money management into a nurturing practice—something that builds you up instead of breaking you down.

Common Pitfalls After a Reset (and How to Avoid Them)

Finishing a 30-day reset is an accomplishment—but it's also a vulnerable moment. Many people stumble after early success, not because they lack discipline, but because old patterns quietly resurface. Anticipating these challenges makes you far more likely to stay on track.

Here are the most common pitfalls—and the strategies to overcome them.

1. The "All-or-Nothing" Trap

After 30 days of focus, some people expect every month to look as perfect as their reset. When a slip happens—an unplanned expense, a missed budget entry—they think, *"I blew it. I'll start over next month."* This all-or-nothing mindset kills momentum.

Solution: Shift to a "next best step" approach. If you overspend one weekend, pause and ask, *"What's one thing I can do today to course-correct?"* Maybe it's bringing lunch from home, skipping a streaming subscription, or simply logging your spending. Success comes from quick recoveries, not flawless execution.

2. Letting the Ritual Fade

During the reset, you had daily challenges and prompts to keep you engaged. Afterward, without structure, it's easy to let reviews slide. A month becomes three months, and suddenly you're back to avoiding your accounts.

Solution: Replace the daily challenge with a recurring ritual. Decide now when your reviews will happen—weekly, biweekly, or monthly—and treat them like appointments. Anchor them to something enjoyable: review your budget while sipping coffee on Saturday mornings, or pair it with a favorite playlist. The ritual keeps momentum alive.

3. Lifestyle Creep

Progress feels good. Maybe you paid off a card or started saving consistently. Then you reward yourself—an upgraded phone, a bigger vacation, or more dinners out. Before long, expenses climb to match income again, and the reset gains disappear.

Solution: Budget for rewards. Build in a "joy" category for fun spending, but keep it proportional to your progress. For example, if you saved $500 this month, allow $50 for a treat. This lets you celebrate without undoing the habits you've built.

4. Money Avoidance Returns

Old emotions don't vanish overnight. Anxiety, guilt, or shame around money may creep back, tempting you to avoid bills or statements. Left unchecked, this avoidance can unravel your reset gains.

Solution: Use the self-compassionate check-in from Section 1. Instead of waiting for avoidance to grow, schedule small, non-threatening money dates—15 minutes to open mail, check balances, or set reminders. Pair these with calming rituals like breathing exercises or tea. The goal is consistency, not intensity.

5. Trying to Do Too Much at Once

After the reset, enthusiasm can tempt you to overhaul *everything*: pay down all debt, max out retirement, start investing aggressively, save for a house. But spreading energy too thin often leads to burnout.

Solution: Focus on one or two key goals at a time. Choose priorities that bring the greatest peace of mind—perhaps building your emergency fund or eliminating one specific debt. Once that habit feels automatic, layer on the next goal. Sustainable change happens step by step.

Reflective Prompt

Take a moment now to write down:

1. Which of these pitfalls feels most likely for you?

2. What's one simple action you'll commit to that will help you avoid it?

By anticipating obstacles, you remove their power. Instead of being derailed, you'll recognize, "Ah, I saw this coming," and calmly redirect your energy back to the habits that work.

Extending the Reset Beyond 30 Days

The 30-Day Reset is designed as a starting point, not a finish line. By now, you've built habits, tested boundaries, and seen how small steps add up. But lasting change comes from weaving those practices into your life long after the 30 days are over. That's where extended resets, quarterly reviews, and annual rituals come in.

Mini-Resets: A Fresh Start Anytime

Life isn't static. Some months will go smoothly; others will feel like setbacks. Instead of waiting until things spiral, use mini-resets as quick recalibrations. A mini-reset might last 7 days or even just a weekend. During that time, you:

- Recommit to tracking expenses daily.
- Pause non-essential spending.
- Reflect on which habits slipped and why.
- Choose one action to re-anchor yourself (e.g., setting up an auto-transfer to savings).

Think of these as "tune-ups" for your financial engine. They're short enough to feel doable but powerful enough to stop small lapses from turning into big setbacks.

Quarterly Reviews: Your 90-Day Checkpoint

Just as businesses review progress every quarter, your financial life benefits from the same rhythm. Every 90 days, set aside an hour to look at:

- **Your numbers:** What changed in income, expenses, savings, debt, and investments?

- **Your emotions:** Did your confidence improve? Did any triggers resurface?

- **Your goals:** Are they still relevant? Do they need adjusting?

At the end of each review, choose one small "reset step" for the next quarter. For example:

- If savings stalled, commit to automating $25 each week.

- If debt progress slowed, call a lender to negotiate a lower interest rate.

- If stress is creeping back, schedule a regular money check-in ritual.

These quarterly reviews prevent drift and keep your momentum aligned with your larger goals.

Annual Financial Retreat: The Big Picture Reset

Once a year, take yourself on a "financial retreat." It doesn't have to be fancy—just a quiet afternoon at home or a day in a coffee shop. The point is to step back and look at the big picture.

During your retreat:

1. **Reflect.** Write about what you learned in the past year—not

just financially, but emotionally. What surprised you? What changed?

2. **Review.** Compare your starting point to where you are now. Celebrate progress, however small.

3. **Reset.** Identify the one or two priorities for the coming year. Avoid overwhelming yourself with a long list.

Many readers find it helpful to tie this retreat to a meaningful moment—like the start of a new year, a birthday, or even the anniversary of when they began their reset. The ritual turns financial growth into an annual tradition that compounds over time.

Real-World Example

Tanya, a single mom, used the 30-Day Reset to get control of her spending. Three months later, she noticed old habits creeping back, so she created her own rhythm: mini 7-day resets whenever she felt off track, quarterly reviews with her sister for accountability, and a quiet December afternoon to reflect on the year. Five years later, she's debt-free, has a healthy savings cushion, and says the rituals kept her grounded even through job changes and emergencies.

Extending the reset isn't about doing more work; it's about building gentle rhythms that support you. Mini-resets, quarterly reviews, and annual retreats are your safety nets, ensuring that financial healing continues long after the first 30 days.

The Role of Identity in Sustaining Success

Habits change behavior in the short term. Identity keeps those changes alive for the long term. After all, it's one thing to say, *"I'm trying to stick to a budget."* It's another to say, *"I'm someone who manages money with confidence."* The second statement is an identity—it changes how you see yourself, and therefore, how you act.

Why Identity Matters

Most people approach money by focusing on outcomes:

- "I want to save $1,000."
- "I want to pay off this credit card."
- "I want to invest for retirement."

These are worthy goals—but they depend on willpower. Once the initial excitement fades, so does momentum. Identity works differently. When you begin to see yourself as *the kind of person who...* builds savings, avoids debt traps, or plans for the future, every decision naturally flows from that self-image.

It's the difference between a runner who says, *"I have to train for this race,"* and one who says, *"I am a runner."* The second doesn't need motivation; the identity itself drives the behavior.

Shaping Your Financial Identity

To make money success stick, you need to shift your story. Start small with these steps:

1. **Choose Your Identity.** Ask: "What kind of person do I want to become with money?" Examples:
    - I am someone who always knows where my money is going.
    - I am someone who saves consistently.

  - I am someone who can talk about money without shame.

2. **Find Evidence.** Each time you act in alignment with this identity—even in a tiny way—write it down. If you transfer $20 to savings, remind yourself, *"I'm a saver."* If you review your budget calmly, note, *"I'm someone who faces money with clarity."*

3. **Repeat and Reinforce.** Identities are built like muscles: through repetition. Every time you live out your new identity, you strengthen it.

The Power of Language

Notice the words you use when you talk to yourself about money. Replace "I should" with "I do." Replace "I'm bad with money" with "I'm learning to manage money better every day." This subtle shift rewires your brain over time.

One reader, Elena, used to say, *"I'm terrible with numbers."* After working through her reset, she started saying, *"I'm someone who manages money thoughtfully."* At first it felt like a stretch, but as she logged progress each month, the identity became reality. Today, she calls herself the "CFO of my household"—a title that motivates her to keep building wealth for her family.

Identity as a Safety Net

Life will throw challenges your way—job changes, emergencies, unexpected expenses. But if your identity is clear, you won't lose your footing. Even if you slip on a budget, you'll return to the path quickly because it's who you are. A saver doesn't abandon saving after one tough month.

Someone who manages money well doesn't stop managing when life gets messy. Identity keeps you grounded through the chaos.

Reflective Prompt

Take five minutes to complete this sentence in your journal:
"With money, I am the kind of person who..."

Write it three different ways, and choose the version that resonates most. Keep this statement somewhere visible—on your phone, mirror, or fridge. Each time you see it, you're reinforcing the identity that will sustain your success.

Building Resilience for the Long Haul

No matter how strong your reset, there will be setbacks. A medical bill arrives. Work slows down. An unexpected family expense pulls cash from savings. Resilience isn't about avoiding these moments—it's about responding in ways that keep you moving forward without undoing all your progress.

1. Expect Setbacks, Don't Fear Them

Too often, people treat setbacks as signs of failure: *"I knew I couldn't stick with this."* But setbacks are not the end of the story—they're part of the process. Every financially secure person you admire has faced challenges and bounced back. The difference is, they planned for recovery.

Reset Mindset: When setbacks happen, replace "I failed" with "I'm resetting." This shifts your focus from shame to strategy.

2. Create Your Resilience Toolkit

A resilience toolkit is a set of practices you turn to whenever things feel shaky. It might include:

- **Financial tools:** an emergency fund, a list of expenses you can cut quickly, or a credit line you only use in crisis.
- **Emotional tools:** breathing exercises, journaling prompts, or a supportive friend you call when stress spikes.
- **Practical steps:** pausing big purchases, scheduling a budget review, or reaching out to a financial coach.

Having these tools identified in advance prevents panic. Instead of reacting impulsively, you'll respond with confidence.

3. Reframe Stress as Data

Financial stress isn't just discomfort—it's information. Maybe your stress shows you that your budget is too tight, your income is too unpredictable, or your goals need adjusting. Instead of avoiding the stress, ask: *"What is this feeling trying to tell me?"*

For example, if you notice dread every time you check your bank account, it may signal that your bills are too close to your paycheck. That's data you can use to adjust timing, build a buffer, or renegotiate payment dates.

4. Build Emotional Recovery Habits

Resilience is just as much about emotional recovery as financial recovery. Simple habits help you bounce back faster:

- **Pause before reacting.** Take three deep breaths before making any money decision under stress.

- **Label the feeling.** Say to yourself, *"I feel anxious,"* or *"I feel overwhelmed."* Naming emotions reduces their intensity.
- **Reconnect to your why.** Remind yourself of the reason you started—whether it's security, freedom, or peace of mind.

5. Focus on the Next Right Step

When problems pile up, it's easy to freeze. Resilience means breaking things into the smallest possible step. Instead of thinking, *"I'll never get out of debt,"* focus on, *"I can make one extra $20 payment this month."* Progress doesn't come from grand gestures—it comes from steady action, even when small.

Real-World Example

James, a teacher, built momentum during his reset but panicked when his car broke down, wiping out his savings. Instead of quitting, he leaned on his toolkit: he cut subscriptions, picked up a tutoring side gig, and restarted his emergency fund at $20 a week. Within six months, not only had he rebuilt savings, but he also felt more confident knowing he could handle setbacks without giving up.

Reflective Prompt

Write down three financial challenges you've faced in the past. For each, note:

- How you responded at the time.
- What worked well.
- What you'd do differently next time.

This reflection reframes past struggles as training for resilience. You'll see that you've already built strength—and you can use those lessons to face whatever comes next.

Designing Your Long-Term Financial Wellness Plan

By now, you've seen how 30 days of focus can spark meaningful change. But financial wellness isn't a one-time reset—it's a lifelong process. To carry your progress forward, you need a plan that blends structure with flexibility. Think of this as your personalized financial blueprint: a living document that grows with you.

1. Anchor Your Core Priorities

Start by naming the three priorities that matter most. These become the pillars of your long-term plan. Examples might include:

- Build and protect an emergency fund.
- Pay down high-interest debt.
- Save consistently for retirement.

Writing these down cements them in your mind. Whenever you feel distracted or overwhelmed, you can come back to your pillars and refocus.

2. Build a System, Not Just Goals

Goals are important, but systems are what keep you moving forward. For example:

- **Goal:** Save $5,000.
- **System:** Automate $100 every paycheck into a high-yield savings account.
- **Goal:** Pay off a credit card.
- **System:** Schedule auto-pay for more than the minimum balance.

Systems reduce the need for daily willpower, making success almost automatic.

3. Create Milestones and Checkpoints

Break big goals into smaller milestones so you can celebrate along the way. Instead of focusing only on becoming debt-free, celebrate every $500 chunk paid down. Instead of waiting until retirement to feel progress, track each $1,000 invested. These checkpoints keep motivation alive and remind you that every step matters.

Schedule regular check-ins:

- Monthly reviews for spending and saving.
- Quarterly reflections on progress toward big goals.

- Annual resets to refine your long-term vision.

4. Keep It Flexible

Life changes, and so will your plan. What matters most is building flexibility into your system. If you lose income, scale back contributions instead of stopping completely. If you earn more, increase savings or debt payments without waiting. Flexibility keeps you from feeling like you've "failed" when circumstances shift.

5. Write Your Financial Vision Statement

A vision statement makes your long-term plan personal. Write 3–5 sentences describing the financial life you want to live. Be specific:

- "I want to live free of credit card debt, with six months of expenses saved, and the ability to travel once a year without stress."
- "I want to feel calm opening my banking app, knowing every dollar has a purpose."

This becomes your compass. When faced with big financial decisions, return to your vision to check if you're moving in the right direction.

6. Connect Money to Meaning

Financial wellness isn't only about numbers—it's about aligning your money with the life you want to live. Ask yourself:

- What do I value most—security, freedom, experiences, family, generosity?
- How can my financial plan reflect those values?

When your plan is tied to meaning, it becomes more than a checklist—it becomes a lifestyle you want to sustain.

Real-World Example

Marcus and Lila, a young couple, wrote a vision statement that included saving for their child's education and taking a family vacation every summer. Their system included auto-saving into a 529 account and setting aside $50 monthly for a "travel jar." They tracked quarterly progress and celebrated each milestone together. Even when unexpected expenses hit, their vision kept them focused on what mattered most.

Reflective Prompt

Write your own **Financial Vision Statement** today. Then, outline three systems you can put in place immediately to support it. Post your vision somewhere visible—on your desk, phone, or bathroom mirror—as a daily reminder of the future you're building.

Your 30-Day Money Reset

Day 26: Write Your Empowered Money Story

Describe, in your own words, the woman you are becoming.
How do you think, act, spend, save, and invest now?
This is your new financial identity — one built from clarity, calm, and self-respect.

Day 27: Release the Old Story

Write down the money beliefs, habits, or fears you've chosen to outgrow.
You don't need to solve them — you only need to decide they no longer

define you.

Letting go is its own kind of power.

Day 28: Choose Your Next Reset

Pick one area to focus on for the next 30 days:

saving, budgeting, debt, investing, or earning.

Choose the path that feels both exciting and supportive.

Day 29: Choose One Action

Select one simple action that will move you forward in your chosen area — and commit to repeating it daily for the next month.

Consistency builds confidence.

Confidence builds wealth.

Day 30: Step Into Your Next Level

End this reset by declaring your next chapter.

What are you ready to create? What are you done tolerating?

What standard are you raising?

This is where your transformation turns into expansion.

You are no longer starting over.

You are moving forward.

Your Final Reset – The Ongoing Cycle of Growth

The 30-Day Money Reset was never designed to be a single sprint. It's a framework you can return to whenever life shifts—whether you're starting a new job, facing unexpected expenses, or simply wanting to re-energize your financial habits. Think of it like strength training: the more often you repeat it, the stronger and more confident you become.

1. Why the Reset Works Repeatedly

Each time you move through 30 focused days, you're not starting from zero—you're reinforcing your identity, habits, and systems. What felt difficult the first time (like saying no to overspending or checking your accounts without anxiety) becomes easier with each round. Repetition transforms these resets into second nature.

2. When to Begin Again

You don't need to wait for a crisis to reset. Ideal times to revisit the 30-day framework include:

- After a major life change (new job, move, relationship shift).
- At the start of a new year or season.
- Anytime you feel yourself drifting from your plan or losing momentum.

The reset serves as a built-in checkpoint—a structured way to pause, reflect, and get back on track.

3. Designing Your Next Cycle

Each round of the reset can have a different focus:

- One cycle might be about building savings.
- Another could focus on cutting debt.
- A later reset might emphasize investing or growing income.

By adjusting the focus each time, you keep momentum alive while layering on new skills.

4. The Compound Effect of Small Resets

The real magic happens when you view these resets not as isolated events, but as building blocks. One round may only move you forward a little—but stacked together over years, the effect compounds into lasting wealth, stability, and peace of mind.

Just as interest grows in an investment account, your consistent resets grow your financial confidence and capability.

5. The Reset as a Lifelong Companion

This book isn't meant to sit on your shelf. It's meant to be lived with—marked up, revisited, and used as a guide whenever you need clarity. The exercises, daily challenges, and reflection prompts are tools you can return to for decades. Every time you do, you'll find new insights because *you* will be in a new stage of life.

Reflective Prompt

Ask yourself: *"If I committed to repeating the 30-Day Reset once every year, where could I be five years from now?"* Write down your answer, and keep it somewhere visible. Let it remind you that this isn't about a single month—it's about building a lifetime of resilience, freedom, and confidence with money.

The Reset is more than a 30-day program—it's a framework you can carry with you for life. Each round builds on the last, layering skills, confidence, and clarity until managing your money feels natural rather than forced. No matter what changes or challenges come your way, you now have a system you can return to—a trusted companion that grows with you. As you close this chapter, know that your financial future is not defined by where you've been, but by the choices you continue to make, one reset at a time.

Chapter Twelve

Conclusion: The Reset Never Ends

You've reached the end of this book, but not the end of your journey. Over the past chapters, you've taken a deep dive into both the **emotional roots** and the **practical steps** of money management, discovering how your past, your psychology, and your daily choices all shape your financial reality.

From the beginning, this book promised you something different: not another set of rigid rules or one-size-fits-all formulas, but a **30-Day Reset framework** you could actually live with. Each chapter gave you daily challenges to test, apply, and repeat — because lasting change doesn't come from theory alone. It comes from action, reflection, and the willingness to try again when life throws you off balance.

Let's pause to recap the ground we've covered:

- You started by uncovering your **money story** — the family narratives, cultural messages, and hidden beliefs that silently influence how you save, spend, or avoid financial decisions. Awareness of those patterns was the first step in rewriting them.

- You then explored the **psychology of money**, learning that financial decisions are rarely about numbers alone. Emotions like fear, guilt, and comparison play a powerful role, but they don't have to control you. With mindful awareness, you began to separate old habits from new possibilities.

- You took a clear-eyed look at your **financial inventory**, asking the honest question: Where am I now? Facing your income, debts, and assets with compassion — not shame — gave you the clarity needed to move forward.

- Through the **Financial Therapy Toolkit**, you practiced exercises that rewired habits and created space for healing. This wasn't about quick fixes; it was about building sustainable, flexible systems that adapt to your life.

- You built a budget that actually works for you — one rooted in **values, not deprivation**. Instead of squeezing yourself into someone else's model, you created a plan that balances essentials, goals, and joy.

- You faced **debt and credit** honestly, reframing them not as enemies but as tools to be managed wisely. By approaching repayment with strategy and self-compassion, you set yourself up for progress without burnout.

- You moved into **saving and investing**, discovering that even the smallest consistent contributions can grow into powerful security and opportunity. Saving became an act of self-care; investing became a path to confidence and long-term freedom.

- You learned how to navigate **financial transitions** — career changes, family shifts, and unexpected challenges — with boundaries and resilience. These moments, once overwhelming, now look like opportunities to reset with clarity and control.

- Finally, you explored how to **sustain success**, weaving financial routines with emotional self-care. You learned to track not just dollars but moods, to celebrate progress both seen and unseen, and to build resilience that keeps you steady through setbacks.

Each step along the way was anchored by your **daily Reset challenges**, small but powerful actions designed to create momentum. Together, they formed more than a checklist — they became proof that progress is possible, no matter your starting point.

And here's the key: this journey isn't a one-off. The *30-Day Money Reset* is a framework you can return to again and again. Whenever you feel stuck, overwhelmed, or ready for the next level, start another cycle. Each time you do, you'll layer new insights on top of old progress. In a year, that could mean twelve focused shifts. Over a lifetime, it means building financial health that grows with you instead of against you.

The truth is, money management is never "done." Life changes. Jobs change. Families change. Your goals, dreams, and challenges will evolve. That's why you now have a system that evolves with you. It's not about chasing perfection; it's about building resilience and agency so that you can handle whatever comes next with confidence.

As you close this book, carry with you three core truths:

1. **Your money story is not fixed.** You have the power to rewrite it, one choice at a time.

2. **Small actions compound.** What feels modest today — a saved $10, a kind budget adjustment, a debt payment made — becomes transformation when repeated over time.

3. **You already have momentum.** By completing this 30-Day

Reset, you've proven that you can take consistent action, and that's the foundation of every future success.

So, what now? You keep resetting. You keep reflecting. You keep choosing the next right step. This isn't about doing everything at once — it's about returning, again and again, to the practice of aligning your money with your values and your future.

The Reset doesn't end here. It begins again with you — today, tomorrow, and every time you decide your financial life deserves care, clarity, and control.

Here's to your next 30 days, and every cycle of growth beyond.

A Roadmap for the Future

This closing roadmap ties everything together. Use it as your guide whenever you want to refocus, restart, or strengthen your financial habits. Think of it as a cycle you can revisit again and again—each round bringing more clarity, stability, and confidence.

Week 1: Awareness and Foundations

- **Day 1–2:** Revisit your money story. Write down one belief from childhood that still influences you. Decide whether it supports or sabotages you.

- **Day 3–4:** Do a fresh financial inventory. List your income, debts, and savings in one place—without judgment.

- **Day 5–7:** Choose one financial boundary to hold this month (e.g., "I won't use credit for non-essentials" or "We'll review shared expenses weekly").

Week 2: Practical Action

- **Day 8–10:** Revisit your budget. Align spending with your values. Adjust one category to reduce stress and increase support.
- **Day 11–12:** Set one small debt goal (e.g., an extra $25 payment). Focus on consistency, not perfection.
- **Day 13–14:** Automate savings. Even $10 per week signals that your future self matters.

Week 3: Growth and Resilience

- **Day 15–16:** Learn one investing concept (compound interest, index funds, retirement accounts). Write down one action you'll take.
- **Day 17–18:** Pair a financial task with a stress reset (deep breathing, a short walk, or journaling).
- **Day 19–21:** Reflect on one setback. Write what you learned and one adjustment to try next time.

Week 4: Integration and Momentum

- **Day 22–23:** Revisit your boundary. Did you hold it? What did it teach you?
- **Day 24–25:** Share one financial win with someone supportive. Speaking progress out loud reinforces growth.

- **Day 26–27:** Write your empowered money story. Describe how your relationship with money has shifted.
- **Day 28–30:** Design your next reset. Choose one clear focus—saving, budgeting, debt, or investing—and commit to one action.

Final Words

This book was designed to give you more than information — it was built to give you a system you can return to again and again. The 30-Day Reset is not about perfection or quick fixes; it's about building resilience, confidence, and clarity that compound with every cycle.

As you close these pages, know this: you are no longer starting from scratch. You've built awareness. You've practiced action. You've proven that change is possible. That proof is yours to keep.

From here, your only job is to keep showing up — 30 days at a time. Each cycle will take you further. Each reset will build on the last. And with every step, you'll strengthen not just your financial life, but your belief in your ability to create lasting security and freedom.

Your next chapter isn't in this book — it's in your daily choices. And now, you're ready.

Here's to your reset, your resilience, and your continued success.

Chapter Thirteen

BONUS SECTION: The Masterclass: From Foundation to Expansion

This section is designed to be revisited once your core habits feel steady.

You have completed the 30-Day Reset. That matters more than you may realize.

Most people spend their entire adult lives cycling through the same financial patterns: periods of good intentions, followed by drift, followed by stress, followed by reaction. They promise themselves they will "get serious" when things calm down, when they earn more, when the kids are older, when the debt is gone, when the next season arrives. But the truth is, there is always another season. There is always another reason to postpone. There is always another excuse dressed up as practicality.

You did something different.

You chose clarity over avoidance. You chose structure over chaos. You chose to learn yourself, not just learn the numbers. You built a foundation of calm, confidence, and consistency around money—something many people never experience, even if they earn a high income.

And now you are ready for the next level.

This is the phase of your financial life where you don't just manage money. You grow it. You multiply it. You direct it. You use it to expand your life in real, meaningful ways.

You shift from "getting on top of your finances" to building sustainable wealth.

You shift from reacting to money to leading it with intention.

You shift from living in a cycle of stress and scarcity to building a life designed around security, opportunity, and personal power.

This bonus section is your guide into that next chapter.

What follows is a curated collection of advanced wealth strategies—practical, modern, and written specifically for women who want more. More stability. More independence. More income streams. More confidence in decision-making. More room to breathe, choose, and expand.

These strategies are not reserved for privileged communities or people who grew up financially educated. They are for the woman who is willing to learn, willing to build, and willing to take herself seriously. They are for you.

Think of this section as the private mentoring session most women never receive. The kind of conversation that usually happens behind closed doors, in rooms where people speak openly about investing, ownership, leverage, risk, and opportunity. Here, the conversation is brought into the light and translated into language that is clear, grounded, and deeply empowering.

Inside this masterclass, you will learn:

How investing can be simple and achievable without becoming your full-time personality.
How real estate can quietly build long-term wealth through structure and patience.
How short-term rentals can turn property into a flexible income engine when managed wisely.
How to think like a wealthy woman without losing your values, softness, or sense of self.
How to identify opportunity with confidence instead of fear.
How to expand your income in ways that feel aligned, sustainable, and real.

But most importantly, you will learn to trust yourself financially.

Because the truth is this:

Wealth is not just about money.
Wealth is about identity.

It is about becoming the woman who sees options instead of limitations. The woman who understands she is capable, resourceful, and worthy of building a strong financial future. The woman who makes decisions from clarity rather than fear. The woman who builds something bigger than today: her freedom, her choices, and her long-term security.

This masterclass is not about becoming someone new.
It is about rising into who you've always been—the woman who simply needed the tools, the knowledge, and the confidence to unlock her full financial power.

You laid the foundation.
Now you build the house.

Part One

How to Grow Your Wealth Automatically and Confidently

Most women were taught to be careful with money.

Save what you can.

Don't take risks.

Avoid debt.

Don't get in over your head.

Be practical.

Be realistic.

Don't want too much.

On the surface, some of that advice sounds sensible. But underneath it, many women absorbed a message that quietly limits financial growth:

"Safety matters more than expansion."

The problem is that safety without growth is not true safety. It's stagnation. It's watching costs rise while your savings sits still. It's working harder each year to maintain the same standard of living. It's feeling like you can never get ahead, no matter how responsible you are.

Here is the truth that changes everything:

Saving protects your present.

Investing secures your future.

A savings account is important. It keeps you stable. It keeps you safe. It gives you breathing room. But savings alone rarely builds long-term wealth. Investing does.

And investing is not reserved for experts.

It doesn't require a finance degree.

It doesn't require six figures.

It doesn't require perfect timing.

It doesn't require you to become someone who checks the market every day.

It requires consistency.

Consistency beats intelligence.

Consistency beats timing.

Consistency beats hype.

Consistency beats fear.

When you understand that, investing becomes far less intimidating and far more empowering. Because you stop believing you have to "get it right." You start understanding you only need to build the habit.

Wealth is built the same way confidence is built: through repeated action.

The Three Investments You'll Use Forever

The investing world is full of noise. Every day there is a new prediction, a new crisis, a new hot trend, a new stock that someone swears will change your life. This noise makes investing feel complicated and risky, especially for women who were never taught how to filter signal from chaos.

So let's simplify it.

There are three core investment categories that form the foundation of most long-term wealth-building strategies. They are simple, timeless, and powerful enough to build wealth quietly in the background of your life.

Index Funds

Index funds are one of the most effective tools available for building long-term wealth. They are not just for beginners. Many experienced investors and professionals still rely heavily on index funds because they are stable, diversified, and low-cost.

An index fund tracks a broad section of the market. Instead of trying to pick "winning" companies, it invests in a wide basket of companies that represent the market itself.

Why that matters is simple: markets historically rise over time. Not every year. Not every month. But over long periods—ten, twenty, thirty years—broad markets have tended to grow. Index funds allow you to participate in that growth without needing to predict anything.

Index funds are powerful for five reasons.

First, diversification. When you buy one index fund, you may instantly own small portions of hundreds or thousands of companies. This spreads risk across industries, sectors, and business cycles. If one company struggles, it barely impacts you. You are not building your future on one bet.

Second, low fees. Index funds are designed to track, not outsmart. That means they don't rely on expensive managers trying to beat the market. Lower costs matter more than most people realize. A tiny difference in fees, compounded over decades, can mean a huge difference in your final wealth.

Third, reliable long-term growth. Markets fluctuate, but over long periods, broad market growth has historically been strong. Index funds are built for the patient investor—the woman who is building, not chasing.

Fourth, simplicity. Index funds don't demand your attention. You can automate contributions and focus on living your life.

Fifth, accessibility. You can build wealth through index funds whether you invest twenty dollars a week or two hundred. It's not the size of the first deposit that matters. It's the habit.

Index funds are the foundation because they are forgiving. They don't punish you for not being perfect. They reward consistency.

ETFs (Exchange-Traded Funds)

ETFs are similar to index funds in many ways, but they trade like stocks. They offer flexibility, transparency, and often even lower fees. For many women, ETFs are the easiest entry point into investing because they feel tangible: you can buy them like a stock, see their price, and understand what you own.

ETFs allow you to invest in broad markets like the S&P 500, international markets, bonds, dividend-focused portfolios, or specific sectors like technology or healthcare.

The advantage of ETFs is that you can tailor your investments without creating complexity. You can choose one or two broad ETFs and still build a diversified portfolio. You can align investments with your values, your risk tolerance, and your timeline.

ETFs are also accessible because many brokerages now allow fractional investing, meaning you can buy part of a share if the full share is expensive. This removes the psychological barrier of thinking you need a lot of money to begin.

The key benefit is that ETFs let you invest with clarity. You can see exactly what the ETF holds. There is no mystery. No hidden strategy. No emotional manipulation. Just a clear, diversified product.

For women building wealth, ETFs are powerful because they combine diversification and simplicity with flexibility.

Blue-Chip Stocks

Blue-chip stocks are large, established companies with long histories of stability. They are the backbone of the stock market. They tend to be well-documented, widely understood, and resilient across economic cycles.

These are not usually the stocks that explode overnight. They are not built for drama. They are built for durability.

Many blue-chip companies pay dividends, which means they distribute a portion of profits to shareholders. Dividends can be reinvested automatically, accelerating compounding over time.

Blue-chip stocks can be a valuable part of a long-term portfolio once your foundation is stable. They can also help you feel connected to what you own because you recognize the brands, understand the business, and can track performance without feeling lost.

The most important principle here is that blue-chip stocks are optional, not required. You can build substantial wealth without ever selecting individual stocks. But for women who want to learn and grow, owning a small number of blue-chips can be a useful step.

Putting It All Together

You do not need dozens of investments. You do not need hours of research. You do not need to follow financial influencers. You do not need to chase trends.

A simple, effective portfolio can be built using:

One to two broad index funds.

One to two ETFs aligned with your goals.

A small handful of blue-chip stocks, only if you want them.

This combination provides diversification, manageable risk, low fees, and simplicity.

And most importantly, it allows automation.

Automation is the secret weapon of wealthy women.

Not because it is clever, but because it removes the need for constant willpower. When you automate investing, you stop relying on motivation. You stop waiting for the perfect month. You stop letting emotions control the timeline. Your money begins working in the background while you build your life.

The Built, Not Born Three-Bucket Wealth System

If investing feels emotionally intimidating, you don't need more information. You need structure.

This framework is designed to create emotional calm and practical clarity.

Bucket One: Safety

This is your cash buffer, emergency fund, and short-term savings. It is not designed for high returns. It is designed for peace. It protects you from panic. It prevents debt. It gives you breathing room.

This bucket supports your nervous system. When life happens, this bucket keeps you stable.

Bucket Two: Stability

This is where long-term compounding happens through index funds and broad ETFs. It is steady. It is boring. It is powerful. This is the bucket that quietly grows your future through time and consistency.

Bucket Three: Growth

This bucket includes individual stocks and advanced opportunities. It is optional and earned. You explore it only when your foundation is secure and your emotional relationship with money is calm enough to tolerate volatility without panic.

When these buckets work together, your financial life becomes structured, stable, sustainable, and scalable. Your wealth grows even during uncertain seasons, not because you predicted the future, but because your system is solid.

The Investing Mindset Shift

Many women were taught that investing is risky. The deeper truth is that investing feels risky because it requires us to tolerate uncertainty. And for women who have lived through instability—financial, emotional, relational—uncertainty can feel threatening.

So let's name it honestly:

Investing is not the same as gambling.

Investing is participation in long-term economic growth.

Investing is building a future where your money does not depend solely on your labor.

What is risky is relying only on savings while costs rise each year.
What is risky is staying financially static for a decade.
What is risky is never giving your money the chance to grow.

When you invest consistently, even small amounts, something changes internally. You stop waiting to feel ready. You start becoming ready through action.

You begin to trust yourself.

Each automated deposit becomes evidence.
Each month you follow through becomes identity.
Each year you stay consistent becomes momentum.

Investing is not about becoming wealthy overnight.
It is about becoming a woman with financial momentum.

And momentum changes everything.

Part Two

Real Estate: Building Wealth Through Ownership

Real estate has created more long-term wealth than almost any other asset class, not because it is glamorous, but because it is built on principles that don't change. Ownership. Demand. Cash flow. Time. Leverage. Compounding.

Real estate is often presented as either intimidating or overly simplified. Some people treat it like an elite club. Others treat it like a get-rich-quick scheme. Both extremes are wrong.

Real estate is a long-term wealth engine. It grows quietly in the background while you live your life. It is not fast money and it is not luck. It is structure, systems, and consistency.

And yes: it is more accessible than most women have been led to believe.

You do not need to be wealthy to begin. You need to be clear.

The Three Wealth Engines of Property

Every property you own can grow your wealth in three ways.

Cash Flow

Cash flow is the rental income left after expenses. It is the part of the property that supports your present-day life: extra breathing room, stability, and income.

Cash flow is not about getting rich. It is about building financial space. Space to make decisions without panic. Space to handle repairs without debt. Space to reinvest.

A good investment property should pay you, not drain you.

Appreciation

Appreciation is the growth in property value over time. It is not guaranteed year to year, but over long periods, many markets grow steadily due to inflation, demand, and development.

Appreciation rewards patience. It is one reason property is powerful: you don't have to do anything to benefit besides owning the asset and maintaining it.

Equity

Equity is the portion of the property you own outright. Each mortgage payment builds equity over time, often assisted by tenants paying rent. Equity is quiet wealth. It doesn't feel exciting day to day. But year to year, it becomes powerful.

Together, cash flow, appreciation, and equity create compounding growth.

The Built, Not Born Property Test

Before purchasing any property, run it through a simple test. This protects you from emotional buying and helps you treat real estate like a business.

First, cash flow. Does the property earn more than it costs when you include mortgage, taxes, insurance, maintenance, vacancy buffer, and management? If it doesn't cash flow, it may still be an asset, but it won't support your financial calm. A wealth-building property should strengthen your life, not tighten it.

Second, condition. Are there structural issues that could become expensive and ongoing? Cosmetic problems are manageable. Structural problems can turn a good deal into a financial drain.

Third, location. Is demand stable? Look for factors that create reliable tenancy: employment hubs, schools, hospitals, infrastructure, low vacancy, population growth. A mediocre property in a strong location can still be a solid investment. A great property in a poor location can become a liability.

This test keeps you grounded. It keeps you disciplined. It keeps you from confusing a "dream home" feeling with an "investment" decision.

Why Women Are Naturally Strong Real Estate Investors

Women often underestimate their natural strengths in property, but many of the traits that build a stable home also build a stable investment.

Women tend to think long-term.
Women tend to notice details.
Women tend to value safety, functionality, and livability.
Women tend to communicate clearly and build trust.

These traits matter. Tenants don't stay because a property is trendy. They stay because it is well managed, well maintained, and feels secure. Those qualities drive stability and stability drives profit.

Real estate is not about being the loudest investor. It is about being the most consistent.

Understanding the Numbers Without Drowning in Them

Real estate math is often presented like a complicated puzzle, but the truth is: you do not need complex spreadsheets to make a strong decision. You need a small number of clear calculations and a commitment to staying conservative.

Think in terms of simple filters:

How much rent can the property realistically earn?
What are the true monthly costs including maintenance and vacancy?
Does the difference leave room for repairs and still create profit?

That's the core.

You can learn advanced metrics over time, but the foundation is clarity. A conservative investor survives and grows. An optimistic investor gets blindsided.

Built, not born means you build your confidence through competence. You learn the numbers. You practice. You get better.

Part Three

Short-Term Rentals: Turning Hospitality into Leverage

Short-term rentals can accelerate wealth when managed well because they combine property ownership with business systems. They are not passive. They are not effortless. But they can be powerful.

And women often excel here for a reason that matters: short-term rental success is built on quality, care, presentation, communication, and consistency—areas where many women naturally have strength.

Short-term rentals are not just extra income. They can be a financial lever. A way to increase cash flow, create flexibility, and generate capital for future investments.

The key is to treat it as a business.

What Makes a Short-Term Rental Profitable

Profitability does not come from having the biggest home. It comes from creating the strongest guest experience.

The first driver is presentation. Your photos are your storefront. Guests decide in seconds. You are not selling a room. You are selling a feeling: cleanliness, comfort, calm, safety, style.

The second driver is cleanliness. Cleanliness is the baseline of trust. Guests forgive small imperfections when a place feels cared for. They do not forgive grime. If you want five-star reviews, cleanliness must be non-negotiable.

The third driver is communication. Great hosts are clear, warm, responsive, and organized. They don't create drama. They create certainty. Certainty makes guests relax. Relaxed guests leave better reviews.

The fourth driver is systems. Successful hosting is not about effort. It is about repeatable processes: checklists, turnover routines, automated messages, restocking habits, pricing rhythm. Systems protect you from burnout and allow scaling.

Scaling Without Losing Yourself

The mistake many women make is scaling too fast without support. They try to do it all and then resent the business they built.

Built, not born means you scale like a leader. You build a team. You outsource cleaning. You create systems. You treat the business like an asset, not a burden.

Scaling can look like raising rates after improving presentation.
Optimizing pricing for weekends and events.
Adding a second property only after the first is stable.
Co-hosting for other owners to earn income without ownership risk.
Reinvesting profits into long-term assets.

Short-term rentals can be powerful, but only when they are structured.

Part Four

The Expansion Mindset: Building Wealth from Calm Power

At this stage of your financial evolution, the most important transformation is not on a spreadsheet. It is in your identity.

Real wealth begins internally, long before it appears externally.

The expansion mindset is what happens when you stop treating wealth as something outside of you—something you fear, chase, or feel unworthy of—and start treating it as something you are built to hold.

You are no longer trying to fix your finances.
You are building your future.

This is the difference between the woman you were and the woman you are becoming.

Outgrowing Scarcity

Scarcity is not simply a lack of money. It is a way of seeing the world. A lens shaped by past experiences, cultural conditioning, and survival moments that taught you to stay small, stay cautious, and stay grateful for whatever you have—even when you are capable of more.

Scarcity whispers that wanting more is dangerous. That ambition makes you selfish. That stability is fragile and should not be tested. It teaches you to prioritize safety over growth, certainty over possibility, and comfort over expansion. Over time, it convinces you that the best you can do is manage what's in front of you rather than build something bigger.

This mindset keeps women in a state of financial vigilance. Always watching. Always bracing. Always preparing for something to go wrong. Even when income increases, scarcity often remains—because the nervous system is still operating from an old rule: *protect, don't expand.*

When you complete the Reset, that rule begins to loosen.

Clarity returns. Not because your life suddenly becomes perfect, but because your relationship with money becomes intelligible. You begin to see patterns instead of chaos. You recognize triggers instead of reacting blindly to them. You understand where your habits came from and, more importantly, how to change them.

Money stops feeling mysterious.
It stops feeling intimidating.
It stops feeling like something that controls you.

You learn that money responds to structure. It responds to consistency. It responds to leadership. When you put systems in place—when you track, plan, automate, and review—money becomes predictable. Not rigid, but responsive. Not emotional, but workable.

This is where scarcity begins to dissolve.

You stop seeing money as something that could disappear at any moment and start seeing it as something that can be built deliberately over time. You move from bracing for loss to planning for growth. From hoping things will improve to knowing how to improve them.

Scarcity loses its grip not because you force it out, but because it no longer matches your lived reality. The stories that once made sense begin to feel outdated. The rules you once lived by start to feel unnecessary.

Scarcity becomes a chapter you remember—not a voice you obey.

And in its place, a new internal orientation forms. One rooted in stability, trust, and self-leadership. You begin to think in longer timeframes. You allow yourself to imagine future versions of your life without immediately dismissing them as unrealistic. You make decisions based on alignment instead of fear.

This is what it means to outgrow scarcity.

Not to deny where you came from.
Not to erase your past.
But to build beyond it.

Your past taught you how to survive.
This phase teaches you how to expand.

Scarcity was never your identity.
It was a response.

And now, you are building something that no longer requires it.

Building from Calm

Many women were taught to manage money through fear. Fear of making mistakes. Fear of being judged. Fear of not having enough. Fear that one wrong decision could undo everything. Over time, this fear-based approach becomes normalized, even praised. Caution is framed as responsibility. Anxiety is mistaken for diligence. Hyper-vigilance is confused with control.

But fear is a poor financial strategy.

Fear narrows your thinking. It leads to avoidance when clarity is needed most. It fuels impulsive decisions meant to relieve discomfort rather than build stability. It creates shame around money instead of confidence, and shame never produces sustainable change.

The expansion mindset builds from a different place.

It builds from calm.

Calm does not mean the absence of anxiety. It does not mean you never question yourself or feel uncertainty. Calm means that anxiety is no longer in charge of your financial system. It means emotions are acknowledged, but decisions are guided by structure, not reaction.

When you build from calm, your financial actions become intentional rather than defensive.

You budget not because you are afraid of losing control, but because clarity creates freedom. A clear budget removes guesswork. It gives you permission to spend, save, and plan without second-guessing yourself. It replaces constant mental calculation with quiet confidence.

You save not because you expect something to go wrong, but because peace of mind is valuable. Savings stop being a symbol of fear and become a foundation of security. You know that whatever happens, you have space to respond instead of panic.

You invest not because you are chasing more, but because you are thinking long-term. Investing becomes an act of trust in yourself and in the future you are building. It is no longer about timing the market or outsmarting anyone. It is about participating consistently and allowing time to do the heavy lifting.

You build wealth not to prove anything, but because wealth creates options. Options to rest. Options to choose. Options to say no. Options to shape your life with intention rather than necessity.

As this mindset takes hold, something subtle but powerful shifts.

Calm becomes your strategy.
Clarity becomes your advantage.
Confidence becomes your identity.

You stop managing money as if it is a constant threat. You start leading it as a system you understand. Decisions feel steadier. Progress feels more predictable. Growth feels earned rather than fragile.

This is the difference between surviving financially and expanding deliberately.

You are no longer reacting to money.
You are directing it.

Increasing Capacity

Most women underestimate not only their ability to earn money, but their ability to *hold* it.

Earning more is often framed as the primary goal, yet many financial struggles persist not because income is too low, but because capacity has not been developed. Capacity is the internal ability to receive, manage, and grow money without fear, guilt, or self-sabotage.

Capacity shows up in quiet, telling ways.

It is your ability to receive money without immediately questioning whether you deserve it.
It is your ability to keep money without feeling compelled to spend it away or justify its existence.
It is your ability to invest money without panicking at normal fluctuations.
It is your ability to watch your account grow without unconsciously finding a way to shrink it again.

When capacity is low, money feels unstable no matter how much of it there is. Gains feel temporary. Growth feels fragile. Success feels like something that could be taken away at any moment.

This is not a character flaw. It is a nervous system response.

Many women learned early that money was unpredictable, emotionally charged, or tied to safety and survival. In those environments, holding more than what felt "safe" could trigger anxiety. So the system learned to stay small, to return to familiar levels, to avoid standing out or risking loss.

As your financial systems strengthen, your internal capacity begins to expand.

Structure teaches your nervous system that money can be predictable. Consistency teaches it that growth does not require constant vigilance. Clarity teaches it that decisions can be made calmly, without urgency or fear.

Over time, numbers that once felt overwhelming become familiar. Decisions that once caused anxiety become manageable. Situations that once triggered panic become moments of assessment rather than reaction.

You stop bracing for loss and start planning for growth.

This is how internal expansion happens. Not through affirmations or forcing confidence, but through repeated evidence that you can handle more than you once believed. Each system you build, each decision you follow through on, each moment you stay grounded instead of reactive increases your capacity.

And as capacity grows, wealth becomes sustainable.

You are no longer relying on willpower to hold onto progress. You are no longer afraid that success will disappear if you relax. You are no longer shrinking yourself to match old comfort zones.

You learn to hold more—financially, emotionally, and practically—without fear.

Your future is bigger than your past.

Not because of luck.
Not because of timing.
Not because you suddenly became a different person.

Because you decided to build differently.

You are becoming a woman who understands money—not theoretically, not someday, not when life calms down, but now. You understand how habits shape outcomes. You understand how systems create stability. You understand how small actions compound.

You are becoming a woman who builds wealth through deliberate choices. Not through hustle. Not through panic. Not through perfection. Through consistency.

And you are becoming a woman whose life expands because she refuses to shrink her dreams to match old circumstances. She builds circumstances that match her dreams.

This is not the end of your journey. It is the beginning of visible transformation.

You will earn more than you once believed was possible, not because you are chasing more, but because your standards have risen and your confidence now supports them. You will save with intention because your money finally has structure and purpose. You will invest with calm, not urgency, because you understand how wealth is built over time—and you trust yourself to follow the process.

You will build a financial life that feels steady, spacious, and strong. One that supports you rather than exhausts you. One that grows quietly in the background while you live fully in the foreground.

Your past is not a prophecy.
It is a starting point.

You are no longer waiting for permission.
You are no longer waiting to feel ready.
You are no longer waiting for someone else to take the lead.

You are taking ownership.

You are choosing consistency over fear.
Structure over chaos.
Progress over perfection.

You are building something deliberate.
Something lasting.
Something entirely your own.

Guided Reflection Pages

Reflection: Who You Were When You Started

Take a moment to remember the woman who opened this book for the first time.

What was she worried about?
What felt heavy, confusing, or overwhelming?
What stories was she carrying about money, herself, or her future?

Write freely here. No editing. No judgment. Just honesty.

Prompt ideas:

When I started this book, my biggest financial stress was...

I believed money was...

I felt most stuck around...

I hoped this book would help me...

Reflection: What Has Shifted

Change doesn't always arrive loudly. Often it arrives quietly — in calmer decisions, softer self-talk, and clearer boundaries.

What feels different now?

Prompt ideas:

The biggest insight I gained was...

One habit I've already changed is...

One belief I no longer carry is...

I now respond differently when money feels stressful because...

Reflection: Evidence of Growth

Confidence isn't a feeling. It's evidence.

List the ways you've already grown — even if they feel small.

Prompt ideas:

I showed up for myself when...

I made a decision I would have avoided before...

I stayed consistent even when it felt uncomfortable by...

I proved to myself that...

Reflection: Your New Financial Identity

You are not the same woman who began this book.

Name who you are becoming.

Prompt ideas:

I am now a woman who...

I trust myself to...

I lead my financial life by...

My relationship with money is becoming...

Reflection: Your Next 30 Days

Growth doesn't stop here. It stabilises through intention.

Prompt ideas:

Over the next 30 days, my focus will be...

One boundary I will protect is...

One system I will strengthen is...

One action I commit to repeating is...

Reflection: A Letter to Your Future Self

Prompt:

Write a letter to yourself six months from now.
Remind her what you've learned.
Tell her what you want her to remember when things get busy or uncertain.
Speak to her with authority, compassion, and confidence.

THE BUILT, NOT BORN MANIFESTO

We are told, quietly and relentlessly, that some women are simply *better with money*.

That they were born confident.

Born disciplined.

Born strategic.

Born lucky.

We are told that wealth belongs to those who "naturally understand it," who grew up around it, who inherited the right knowledge, the right mindset, the right start.

This is a lie.

Wealth is not something you are born into.

It is something you **build**.

Not through perfection.

Not through privilege.

Not through flawless decisions.

But through awareness.

Through structure.

Through repetition.

Through courage.

Through choosing yourself again and again.

Built, not born.

We Reject the Myth of the "Naturally Wealthy Woman"

There is no gene for financial confidence.

There is no personality type reserved for stability, abundance, or calm control.

There is only exposure, education, and practice.

Most women were never taught how money actually works.

They were taught to be careful.

To avoid risk.

To feel grateful for "enough."

To outsource decisions.

To shrink their desires to match what felt safe.

None of that makes you bad with money.

It makes you **untrained**.

And training can be learned.

We Honor Where We Started — Without Letting It Define Us

Your past does not disqualify you.

Not debt.

Not mistakes.

Not avoidance.

Not fear.

Not starting late.

Not starting from zero.

Every woman builds from wherever she stands.

Some start with knowledge.

Some start with resilience.

Some start with necessity.

Some start with hunger.

Some start with nothing but determination.

There is no shame in your starting point.

There is power in your decision to move forward.

We Build Wealth Through Structure, Not Shame

Shame does not create discipline.

Fear does not create consistency.

Self-criticism does not create confidence.

Structure does.

Clear systems.

Repeatable habits.

Gentle accountability.

Calm decision-making.

We stop punishing ourselves for what we didn't know before we knew better.

We stop making money a moral test.

We build systems that support us — not ones that break us.

We Choose Consistency Over Intensity

We do not need to overhaul our lives overnight.

We do not need to be perfect for thirty days straight.

We do not need to "fix everything" to be worthy of progress.

We build wealth the way real stability is built:

One decision at a time.

One habit at a time.

One reset at a time.

Small actions, repeated, change everything.

We Understand That Wealth Is Identity Work

Money follows identity.

Not income.

Not intelligence.

Not hustle.

Identity.

When you see yourself as capable, you act differently.

When you see yourself as someone who plans, you follow through.

When you see yourself as someone who builds, you stop sabotaging.

This work is not about becoming someone else.

It is about removing the layers that told you who you weren't.

We Build from Calm, Not Chaos

We do not build wealth from panic.

We do not make decisions from urgency.

We do not treat money like an emergency unless it truly is one.

Calm is not passivity.

Calm is power under control.

Calm allows clarity.
Clarity allows strategy.
Strategy allows growth.

We lead our finances — they do not lead us.

We Expand Without Apology

We allow ourselves to want more.

More stability.
More freedom.
More options.
More time.
More peace.

Not because we are greedy.

But because expansion is human.

We release the belief that wanting more makes us selfish.

We understand that when women build wealth, families stabilize, communities strengthen, and futures expand.

We Trust the Woman We Are Becoming

We stop waiting to feel "ready."

Readiness is built through action, not before it.

Each decision strengthens trust.
Each boundary builds confidence.
Each reset reinforces identity.

We no longer ask, *Can I do this?*

We ask, *What's my next step?*

We Are Built, Not Born

We are built by:

choosing clarity over avoidance

choosing structure over chaos

choosing consistency over perfection

choosing growth over fear

choosing ourselves over old stories
You are not lucky.
You are intentional.
You are not behind.
You are building.

And everything you create from here forward is the result of conscious design — not chance.

The Wealth Identity Declaration

Who I Am. What I Create. What I No Longer Settle For.

This declaration is not an affirmation.
It is a decision.
A standard.
A new identity you step into — fully, unapologetically, and permanently.
Read it slowly.
Return to it often.
Own every word.

I am a woman who leads myself with clarity and intention.

I no longer operate from confusion, avoidance, or fear.
I face my finances with honesty, strength, and steadiness.
My decisions are thoughtful, grounded, and aligned with who I am becoming.

I am a woman who builds wealth, not by accident but by design.

I use systems, strategies, and structure.
I save consistently.
I invest wisely.
I create stability and opportunity through the choices I make every day.
My wealth is built through deliberate action — not luck, not chance, not waiting for the perfect moment.

I am a woman who understands money and is no longer intimidated by it.

Money is not chaos.
Money is not a mystery.
Money is not something I fear or mismanage.
It is a tool I control.
It is a resource I direct.
It is a partner in the life I am building.

I am a woman who takes responsibility without shame and moves forward without hesitation.

I release old mistakes.
I outgrow old patterns.
I forgive myself for what I didn't know.
I stand firmly in what I know now — and I build from here.

I am a woman who expects abundance because I create it.

I expect stability because I build it.
I expect opportunity because I pursue it.
I expect growth because I commit to it.
I no longer shrink my goals to fit my comfort zone.
I expand my actions to meet my potential.

I am a woman whose financial life supports her, strengthens her, and gives her freedom.

Wealth is not about status.
It is about safety, independence, options, and peace.
I am creating a life where my financial decisions come from vision, not fear.
From confidence, not pressure.
From possibility, not limitation.

I am a woman who rises, evolves, and expands — without apology.

I hold myself to higher standards.
I choose long-term over impulsive.

I choose clarity over chaos.
I choose growth over stagnation.
My wealth reflects who I am becoming —
focused, capable, intentional, and powerful.

This is my identity now.

I am a woman who understands money.
I am a woman who builds wealth.
I am a woman whose life is expanding.
And from this moment forward, I act like her, decide like her, earn like her,
and build the future she deserves.

A Final Note from the Author

If you've reached this page, you've done something extraordinary—something most people will never choose to do. You confronted your financial life with honesty. You built new skills with intention. And you chose to lead yourself into a stronger future instead of waiting for one to arrive.

That matters.

In fact, it changes everything.

I wrote this book because I know what it feels like to start from nothing. I know what it feels like to want more for your life but not know where to begin. And I know how overwhelming money can feel when you've never been taught the systems, the language, or the mindset behind it.

But I also know what becomes possible when you take ownership of your finances—even one small step at a time.

You gain clarity.

You gain confidence.

You gain control.

And those three things together change the trajectory of your life.

My hope is that this book doesn't just give you information—it gives you identity.

The identity of a woman who understands money.
A woman who builds wealth intentionally.
A woman who doesn't shrink herself to fit her past but rises to meet her future.

Where you go from here is entirely up to you.
You can revisit the resets anytime you need a refresh.
You can take the next step in investing, real estate, or business ownership.
You can expand your income, your confidence, your opportunities, and your vision.

Just remember this: wealth is not reserved for women who were raised with it.
It belongs to the women who decide to build it.

You have already proven that you are one of those women.

Thank you for allowing me to be part of your journey.
I am cheering for your next chapter—because I know it will be bigger, clearer, and more powerful than anything that came before.

You are capable.
You are ready.
And your future is already expanding.

— *Michelle Ward*

Resources & Further Reading

A Curated Library for Your Ongoing Financial Growth

The journey you've begun in this book doesn't end with the final page. Financial confidence, emotional resilience, and long-term wealth are built through continued learning, reflection, and exposure to ideas that challenge old patterns and reinforce new ones.

The resources below are not meant to overwhelm you or suggest that you need "more information" to be worthy or capable. Rather, they are offered as trusted companions — books, tools, and references you can return to as your financial life evolves.

This list is intentionally selective, not exhaustive. Each recommendation aligns with the philosophy of this book: practical, human, psychologically informed, and grounded in real-world application.

Use these resources slowly. You don't need to read everything at once. Let them meet you where you are.

Money & Psychology

Understanding the Emotional Roots of Financial Behavior

These books explore how beliefs, emotions, habits, and cognitive biases shape financial decisions — often more powerfully than logic or math.

The Psychology of Money — Morgan Housel
A modern classic that explains why people behave irrationally with money, even when they "know better." This book reinforces one of the core messages of *Built, Not Born*: financial success is less about intelligence and more about behavior, patience, and long-term thinking.

Mind Over Money: Overcoming the Money Disorders That Threaten Our Financial Health — Brad Klontz & Ted Klontz
Written by pioneers in financial psychology, this book explores how childhood experiences and emotional wounds can quietly sabotage financial progress. It's particularly useful if you've ever felt stuck repeating the same money patterns despite good intentions.

Financial Recovery: Developing a Healthy Relationship with Money — Karen McCall
A compassionate guide for those rebuilding after financial stress, shame, or loss. This book emphasizes gentleness, awareness, and gradual change — values that align closely with the Reset framework.

Scarcity: Why Having Too Little Means So Much — Sendhil Mullainathan & Eldar Shafir
A research-based exploration of how scarcity affects decision-making, focus, and self-control. This book helps explain why "just trying harder" rarely works — and why systems matter more than willpower.

The Financial Wisdom of Ebenezer Scrooge — Rick Kahler, Ted Klontz & Dick Wagner
A short, reflective read that blends storytelling with financial psychology, showing how transformation happens when awareness meets intention.

Foundational Personal Finance

Principles That Stand the Test of Time

These books provide solid frameworks for managing money in ways that support freedom, values, and long-term stability.

Your Money or Your Life — Vicki Robin & Joe Domínguez

A values-based approach to money that encourages intentional spending and conscious living. This book is ideal if you want your financial decisions to align with meaning, not just accumulation.

The Millionaire Next Door — Thomas J. Stanley & William D. Danko

Based on extensive research, this book dismantles myths about wealth and highlights the quiet, consistent behaviors that actually build it.

The Total Money Makeover — Dave Ramsey

While not every strategy will resonate with every reader, this book offers a clear, structured approach to debt elimination and financial discipline. Use it selectively, without guilt or rigidity.

I Will Teach You to Be Rich — Ramit Sethi

A modern, practical guide focused on automation, conscious spending, and building a financial life that feels enjoyable, not restrictive.

The Latte Factor — David Bach

A simple reminder of how small, consistent choices compound over time. Best read as inspiration rather than strict instruction.

Saving & Investing

Building Wealth with Simplicity and Confidence

These resources demystify investing and reinforce the idea that long-term wealth is accessible, not exclusive.

The Simple Path to Wealth — JL Collins

A clear, no-nonsense introduction to long-term investing, particularly index funds. Ideal for readers who want straightforward guidance without complexity.

Broke Millennial Takes On Investing — Erin Lowry

A friendly, approachable investing guide written specifically for those who feel late to the game or overwhelmed by financial jargon.

Stock Investing for Women — Rob Maxwell

A practical introduction to stock market fundamentals, written with clarity and confidence for women building long-term portfolios.

Common Sense on Mutual Funds — John C. Bogle

A foundational text on low-cost, long-term investing from the founder of Vanguard. Best for readers who want to understand the philosophy behind index investing.

Financial Therapy & Emotional Wellbeing

Where Money and Mental Health Intersect

These works explore the connection between emotional regulation, leadership, resilience, and financial wellbeing.

Financial Therapy: Theory, Research, and Practice — Bradley T. Klontz, Sonya L. Britt & Kristy L. Archuleta

A more academic resource that underpins many of the concepts introduced in this book. Ideal for readers who want a deeper understanding of the research behind financial behavior change.

Happy Money: The Science of Happier Spending — Elizabeth Dunn & Michael Norton

Explores how spending choices affect happiness and fulfillment, reinforcing the idea that money is a tool — not a goal.

Dare to Lead — Brené Brown

Not a finance book, but a powerful resource for building courage, boundaries, and self-trust — all essential to financial leadership and decision-making.

Practical Tools & Apps

Support Systems for Everyday Life

Tools are not a substitute for mindset, but the right ones can reduce friction and support consistency.

YNAB (You Need a Budget)

A proactive budgeting app designed to help you plan ahead rather than track past mistakes.

Mint

A free budgeting and expense-tracking tool with alerts and summaries. Best for visibility and awareness.

Goodbudget

A digital envelope system that supports mindful spending and shared financial planning.

Betterment / Wealthfront

Beginner-friendly robo-advisors that automate investing based on your goals and risk tolerance.

Morningstar

An independent source for investment research and analysis, useful as your confidence grows.

Websites & Free Guides

Reliable, Plain-Language Education

Consumer Financial Protection Bureau (CFPB)

Clear, unbiased guides on credit, debt, mortgages, and consumer rights.

National Endowment for Financial Education (NEFE)

Free educational resources, worksheets, and workshops focused on financial literacy.

Investopedia

A comprehensive reference for financial terms and concepts. Use it as a dictionary, not a roadmap.

Khan Academy – Personal Finance

Free video lessons covering budgeting, credit, investing, and taxes.

NerdWallet

Helpful comparisons of financial products, calculators, and decision guides.

A Final Note on Learning

You do not need to master everything here to be financially capable or successful. Knowledge compounds best when paired with action, reflection, and patience.

Return to these resources when:

You feel curious, not pressured

You're entering a new financial season

You want to deepen, not overhaul, what you've built

Your financial life is not built in one book or one year. It is built, steadily and intentionally, over time.

Acknowledgements

Writing a book is never a solo act, and **Built, Not Born** is no exception.

First, to the women who show up with courage, curiosity, and a willingness to transform their lives—you are the heartbeat of this book. Your stories, your frustrations, your breakthroughs, and your honesty shaped every chapter. You are the reason this work exists, and the reason it continues to grow.

To my family—thank you for your patience during the long writing days, the late-night editing sessions, and the endless cups of coffee. Thank you for cheering me on when I questioned myself, for grounding me when life became chaotic, and for reminding me to practice the very resets I write about. You are my foundation, always.

To my closest friends, thank you for believing in me long before I believed in myself. Your encouragement, humor, and unwavering support have lifted me through every stage of this journey.

To the mentors, teachers, and financial guides who helped shape my understanding of money—not just as numbers, but as a deeply emotional, personal, and powerful force—your insight gave this book its balance of heart and strategy. Your wisdom helped me see that money doesn't just change circumstances; it changes identities.

And finally, a note from me, Michelle:

I didn't grow up with wealth, privilege, or a road map. I built my life one determined step at a time—raising a family, creating businesses from scratch, writing hundreds of books, and building a publishing empire piece by piece. I learned through mistakes, resilience, and a relentless commitment to creating something better.

If you're holding this book, I want you to know something important:

You don't need a perfect past, perfect habits, or perfect circumstances to create a rich life.

You just need a starting point—and the willingness to begin.

Thank you for choosing this 30-day journey.

Thank you for choosing *yourself*.

My hope is that these pages give you clarity, courage, and the confidence to rewrite your money story in a way that feels powerful, peaceful, and deeply yours.

— **Michelle Ward**

About the author

Michelle Ward is a bestselling author, entrepreneur, and the founder of Harbor & Ink Press—one of the fastest-growing independent publishing brands in personal development, finance, and lifestyle. What began as a one-woman project has evolved into a multi-imprint publishing powerhouse with more than 140 titles across self-help, money management, cookbooks, kids' nonfiction, journals, and speciality puzzle books.

Michelle's career is rooted in grit, reinvention, and self-education. She didn't come from wealth—she built it. From launching her first books on a shoestring budget to growing a thriving publishing company and an expansive real-estate portfolio, Michelle has spent years mastering the habits, mindsets, and systems that create long-term financial stability and freedom.

Her books range from Airbnb how-to guides and personal finance titles to children's fact books, puzzle books, cookbooks, and guided journals. Across every genre, her work is practical, clear, beautifully designed, and deeply relatable—created for readers who want real change, not just theory.

Through Harbor & Ink Press, Michelle has reached thousands of readers seeking clarity, confidence, and direction in their financial lives. Her mission is simple:

make money management feel doable, empowering, and acces-

sible for everyday people—especially women who are rebuilding their financial identity and stepping into their next chapter.

Built, Not Born is Michelle's most personal project yet: an emotional and practical 30-day reset designed to help women understand their money story, build systems that stick, and create a financial life grounded in confidence instead of chaos.

When she's not writing, Michelle is developing new publishing projects, managing her real-estate ventures, or creating tools that help women rewrite their money story and build a life that feels rich in every sense of the word.

Reference List

Reference List

15 types of healthy boundaries and how to communicate them. (2023,June 15). Center for Mindful Therapy.https://mindfulcenter.org/15-types-of-healthy-boundaries-and-how-to-communicate-them/

20 Expert Tips OnHow To Manage Crisis Situations - Sash And Company.(2024, July 13). Sashandcompany.com.https://sashandcompany.com/crisis-management/how-to-manage-crisis-situations/

(2023). Massmutual.com.https://blog.massmutual.com/planning/blended-family-budgeting

5 Strategies toOvercome Financial Self-Sabotage. (2022). PsychologyToday.https://www.psychologytoday.com/us/blog/mental-wealth/202209/5-strategies-overcome-financial-self-sabotage

A phenomenologicalstudy of family influence on Millennial college students' money beliefs andbehaviors - ProQuest. (2025). Proquest.com.https://search.proquest.com/openview/f50c3fead3d60a9ee3d7f347dcc149ce/1?pq-origsite=gscholar&cbl=18750

Aksu, Ç., & Ayar, D. (2022, October). *The effects of visualization meditation onthe depression, anxiety, stress and achievement motivation levels of nursingstudents.* Nurse Education Today. https://doi.org/10.1016/j.nedt.2022.105618

A Step-by-StepGuide to Effective Budgeting - Haven Financial Planning. (2024, July 30). Haven Financial Planning.https://havenfinancialplanning.co.uk/a-step-by-step-guide-to-effective-budgeting/

Ayoola, E. (2024, February 20). *The 7 Best Budget Apps for 2021.* NerdWallet.https://www.nerdwallet.com/article/finance/best-budget-apps

Brown, M., Henchoz, C., & Spycher, T. (2018, June). *Culture and financial literacy: Evidencefrom a within-country language border.* Journal of Economic Behavior &Organization. https://doi.org/10.1016/j.jebo.2018.03.011

Benson, A. (2022, March 14). *What Is ESG Investing and How Does It Compare?* NerdWallet.https://www.nerdwallet.com/article/investing/esg-investing

Carey, E. (2023, May 18). *How to Rewire Your Brain for a Positive Money Mindset.* Medium.https://medium.com/@EmmaCarey.Writer/how-to-rewire-your-brain-for-a-positive-money-mindset-a59990934a11

Consumer Financial Protection Bureau. (2024). *An essential guide to building an emergencyfund.* Consumer Financial Protection Bureau.https://www.consumerfinance.gov/an-essential-guide-to-building-an-emergency-fund/

Chen, J. (2024, April 16). *Investing for Beginners: A Guide to Assets.* Investopedia.https://www.investopedia.com/articles/basics/11/3-s-simple-investing.asp

Coachingly. (2024). Coachingly.ai.https://www.coachingly.ai/blog/single/the-intersection-of-health-wellness-and-financial-empowerment

Dealing withFinancial Anxiety: How to Decrease Stress Around Money > 1st United CreditUnion. (n.d.). Www.1stunitedcu.org.https://www.1stunitedcu.org/more-for-you/financial-wellness/dealing-with-financial-anxiety--how-to-decrease-stress-around-money

Exploring KeyFinancial Considerations for Career Change. (2025,April 16). ProfileTree Web Design and Digital Marketing.https: //profiletree.com/financial-considerations-for-career-change/

Finnerty, K. (2024, September 26). *Fear, Self-Sabotage, and Money: Understanding the PsychologicalBarriers to Financial Success.* Medium.https://medium.com/@Kevin_Finnerty_Gabagool/fear-self-sabotage-and-money-understanding-the-psychological-barriers-to-financial-success-e7b1c511234c

Gregoire, C. (2018, February 8). *How Money Changes the Way You Think and Feel.* Greater GoodMagazine.https://greatergood.berkeley.edu/article/item/how_money_changes_the_way_you_think_and_feel

Gush Admin. (2024, December 19). *7-Step Exercise with Free Wheel of Life Template for Coaching.*Simply.Coach.https://simply.coach/blog/exercise-wheel-of-life-template-coaching/

Hung, J. (2025, February 25). *The Neuroscience of Risk: How Our Brains Process Financial Uncertainty.*Jaron Hung.https://www.jaronhung.com/the-neuroscience-of-risk-how-our-brains-process-financial-uncertainty/

How Clients' MoneyScripts Predict Their Financial Behaviors. (n.d.).Financial Planning Association.https://www.financialplanningassociation.org/article/journal/NOV12-how-clients-money-scripts-predict-their-financial-behaviors

Impulse Buying AndMoney Challenges: Understanding Emotional Spending | BetterHelp. (2025, February 13). Betterhelp.com ; BetterHelp.https://www.betterhelp.com/advice/stress/impulse-buying-and-money-challenges-understanding-emotional-spending/

Jenn. (2024, March 22). *Navigating Finances Together: Financial Tips for Couples - MechanicsCooperative Bank.* Mechanics Cooperative Bank -.https://mechanics-coop.com/navigating-finances-together-financial-tips-for-couples/

Koshy, K. (2017, June 15). *Reflective Practice in Health Care and How to Reflect Effectively*.International Journal of Surgery Oncology.https://doi.org/10.1097/IJ9.0000000000000020

Landers, L. (2024, May 27). *Love, Money, and Attachment: How it All Connects*. LeBaron-Black.https://lebaron-black.byu.edu/love-money-and-attachment-how-it-all-connects

Mendelsohn, A. I. (2019, June 1). *Creatures of Habit: The Neuroscience of Habit and Purposeful Behavior*.Biological Psychiatry. https://doi.org/10.1016/j.biopsych.2019.03.978

MyFICO. (2016). *Howare FICO Scores Calculated? | myFICO*. Myfico.com.https://www.myfico.com/credit-education/whats-in-your-credit-score

Nissen, S., Hayward, B., & McManus, R. (2019). *Student Debt and Wellbeing: a ResearchAgenda*. Kōtuitui: New Zealand Journal of Social Sciences Online.https://doi.org/10.1080/1177083x.2019.1614635

Neff, K. D. (2023). *Self-Compassion:Theory, Method, Research, and Intervention*. Annual Review of Psychology.https://doi.org/10.1146/annurev-psych-032420-031047

Neidel, C. (2022, April 26). *Needs vs. wants: How to budget for both*. NerdWallet.https://www.nerdwallet.com/article/finance/financial-needs-versus-wants

Request. (2025, February 14). *Money Journaling: A New Approach to Understanding Your Spending Habits| IV Capital*. IV Capital | Global Trading & Real Estate.https://iv-capital.com/articles/money-journaling-a-new-approach-to-understanding-your-spending-habits/

Ryu, S., & Fan, L. (2022, February 1). *The Relationship between Financial Worriesand Psychological Distress among U.S. Adults*. Journal of Family andEconomic Issues. https://doi.org/10.1007/s10834-022-09820-9

Robinson, L., & Smith, M. (2020, May 14). *Coping with Financial Stress - HelpGuide.org*.HelpGuide.org.https://www.helpguide.org/mental-health/stress/coping-with-financial-stress

Sutton, J. (2018, May 14). *5 Benefits of Journaling for Mental Health*. Positive Psychology.https://positivepsychology.com/benefits-of-journaling/

Snowball vs.Avalanche Method for Paying Down Debt. (2024). NavyFederal Credit Union.https://www.navyfederal.org/makingcents/credit-debt/snowball-vs-avalanche-for-paying-down-debt.html

Sibley, L. (2023, October 5). *Eight types of budgeting processes and the pros and cons of each*.Bedford Consulting.https://bedfordconsulting.com/eight-types-of-budgeting-processes-and-the-pros-and-cons-of-each/

Schoen, A. (2025, March 27). *Audrey Schoen, LMFT*. Audrey Schoen, LMFT.https://www.audreylmft.com/blogs/financial-therapy-programs

Stoewen, D. L. (2017). *Dimensions of wellness: Change your habits, change your life*. TheCanadian Veterinary Journal. https://pmc.ncbi.nlm.nih.gov/articles/PMC5508938/

The Psychology ofMoney: Understanding the Emotional Side of Finances and How It Affects YourDecisions. (2024). Nasdaq.com.https://www.nasdaq.com/articles/psychology-money-understanding-emotional-side-finances-and-how-it-affects-your-decisions

Understanding andOvercoming Financial Anxiety. (2025, April 16). Anxiety Training. https://anxietytraining.com/overcoming-financial-anxiety/

What to know aboutthe debt snowball vs avalanche method — Wells Fargo.(n.d.) . Www.wellsfargo.com.https://www.wellsfargo.com/goals-credit/smarter-credit/manage-your-debt/snowball-vs-avalanche-paydown/

Printed in Dunstable, United Kingdom

91222423R00139